THE AMERICAN NEGRO

HIS HISTORY AND LITERATURE

THE

FREE NEGRO FAMILY

E. Franklin Frazier

10236

ARNO PRESS and THE NEW YORK TIMES

NEW YORK 1968

General Editor
WILLIAM LOREN KATZ

THE NEARLY 500,000 FREE NEGROES IN THE UNITED STATES AT the outbreak of the Civil War, half of them in the South, included many who were "well-to-do," who tended to develop a stable and patriarchal pattern of family life which was fully comparable to that of the slave-holding whites. The continuing strength of such families became evident in the course of E. Franklin Frazier's study, *The Negro Family in Chicago,* published in 1932, and led to his second book, *The Free Negro Family,* which appeared in the same year.

The stories of selected free Negro families are here recounted against the background of the entire free Negro population—its origins, development and distribution, and the characteristics of free Negro communities. In this analysis—and even more explicitly in subsequent works—Frazier's studies of the specific experiences of the Negro are also illustrative of more general sociological relationships. As Ernest W. Burgess once noted, Frazier's work on the Negro family has outstanding significance "for the understanding of the family in general . . ."

E. Franklin Frazier (1894-1962) was born in Baltimore, Maryland, and was educated at Howard University, Clark University, the New York School of Social Work, and the University of Chicago, where he received a Ph.D. degree. His academic experience included teaching and administrative positions in public and private schools in several southern states; the directorate of the Atlanta School of Social Work for five years; and a professorship of sociology at Morehouse College, Fisk University, and (for twenty-five years) Howard University, where he was chairman of the Department of Sociology.

Dr. Frazier held research positions with the University of Chicago, the Social Science Research Council, and Mayor La Guardia's Commission on Conditions in Harlem, following the 1935 race riot. He was a Guggenheim Fellow for the study of the Negro family in Brazil and the West Indies, President of the American Sociological Association, chairman of UNESCO's committee of experts on race and chief of its Applied Science Division in Paris. Among his other books are *The Negro Family in the United States, Negro Youth at the Crossways, The Negro in the United States,* and (originally published in France) *Black Bourgeoisie.*

Doxey A. Wilkerson
ASSOCIATE PROFESSOR OF EDUCATION
YESHIVA UNIVERSITY

THE FREE
NEGRO FAMILY

PRINTED BY BAIRD-WARD PRINTING COMPANY
NASHVILLE, TENNESSEE

THE
FREE NEGRO FAMILY

*A Study of Family Origins
Before the Civil War*

By

E. FRANKLIN FRAZIER

Professor of Sociology, Fisk University

AUTHOR OF "THE NEGRO FAMILY IN CHICAGO"

FISK UNIVERSITY PRESS
NASHVILLE, TENNESSEE
1932

To

C. S. BROWN

AND HIS LAMENTED WIFE

AMAZA DRUMMOND

AUTHOR'S PREFACE

The materials presented in this study form a part of a comprehensive study of the Negro family which is being carried on as one of the major projects of the Social Science Department of Fisk University. This project is a continuation of the writer's researches which were published in a recent volume under the title, THE NEGRO FAMILY IN CHICAGO.[1] In his first study the writer undertook to measure the changes in the Negro family, resulting from urbanization, in relation to the economic, social, and cultural organization of the Negro community in the city. As a result of this approach to the study of the problem it was shown among other things that those families with a heritage of traditions and economic competency extending back before the Civil War have constantly played a stabilizing rôle in the population as the Negro has been compelled to make adjustments to our changing civilization. It is the purpose of the present study to show in a more thoroughgoing fashion how these families originated and became the vanguard in the cultural and economic progress of the race. It is hoped that this study will give a larger background for an understanding of the relation of cultural factors to the problems of the urban Negro family which formed the subject of the volume already published. It does not pretend to offer a comprehensive account of the free Negro families before the Civil War, but gives the career of typical families in the free Negro communities that developed in relation to the ecological organization of slavery. This approach, which related the career of the Negro family to the economic and cultural life of America, is the same as that of the larger study in progress, dealing with the changes in the Negro family in modern industrial society.

[1] University of Chicago Press, 1932.

The writer is indebted to the Social Science Research Council for the initial grant which made possible the undertaking of the larger study as a part of the social research program at Fisk University.

E. Franklin Frazier.

Fisk University, May 2, 1932.

CONTENTS

TABLES

MAPS

CHAPTER I.

ORIGIN, GROWTH, AND DISTRIBUTION OF THE FREE NEGROES

A class of free Negroes existed in America almost from the time that they were first introduced into the Virginia colony in 1619. Contrary to popular belief, the free class may even be said to be prior in origin to the slave class, since the first Negroes brought to America did not have the status of slaves, but of indentured servants.[1] Contracts of indentured Negro servants indicate that the status of the first Negroes was the same as that of the white servants.[2] Moreover, court records show that Negroes were released originally upon the completion of a term of servitude. The slave status, for which the white colonists had no model in England, "developed in customary law, and was legally sanctioned at first by court decisions."[3] Although it was not until 1662 that the first act of the Virginia slave code was passed, slavery by this time had apparently become established in practice.[4] As early as 1651 we find a Negro, Anthony Johnson, who was probably enumerated among the indentured servants in the census of 1624, having assigned to him in fee simple a land patent for two hundred and fifty acres of land.[5] Two years later this same man was the defendant in a suit brought against him by another Negro for his freedom from servitude, after having served "seaven or eight years of Indenture."[6] According to Russell, "The upper limit of the period in which it was possible for

---

[1]John H. Russell, *The Free Negro in Virginia* (Baltimore, 1913), p. 29. See also Ulrich B. Phillips, *American Negro Slavery* (New York, 1927), p. 75.

[2]Phillips, op. cit., p. 75.

[3]Russell, op. cit., pp. 18-19. See Phillips, op. cit., p. 75.

[4]Ibid., p. 19.

[5]Ibid., p. 25.

[6]Ibid., p. 32.

1

negroes to come to Virginia as servants and to acquire freedom after a limited period is the year 1682."[7] Nevertheless, the free class continued to grow until the Civil War.

The free Negro population was increased through five sources: (1) children born of free colored persons; (2) mulatto children born of free colored mothers; (3) mulatto children born of white servants or free women; (4) children of free Negro and Indian parentage; (5) manumitted slaves.[8] The increase in the free Negro population through the offspring of free colored parents, though difficult to estimate, contributed to the growth of this class until Emancipation. Likewise, the numerous cases of off-springs from white fathers and free colored mothers would indicate that from this source the free Negro population was constantly enlarged.[9] Mulattoes born of white servant women and free white women were also a significant factor, for it was soon the cause for special legislative action. Virginia, in 1691, passed a law prescribing that "any white woman marrying a negro or mulatto, bond or free," should be banished.[10] Maryland, in 1681, provided in an act that children born of white servant women and Negroes were free. Eleven years later any white woman who married or became the mother of a child by either a slave or free Negro became a servant for seven years.[11] Pennsylvania found it necessary to restrict the intermarriage of Negroes and whites through legislative action in 1725-1726, after having punished a woman for "abetting a clandestine marriage between a white woman and a negro" in 1722.[12] This restriction was swept away, as well as the other restrictions upon the Negro, in 1780.[13] Seemingly, mixed marriages became common, for Thomas Branagan complained:

> There are many, very many blacks who . . . begin to feel themselves consequential . . . will not be satisfied unless they get white

[7]Ibid., p. 39.
[8]Ibid., pp. 40-41.
[9]Carter G. Woodson, *Free Negro Heads of Families in the United States in 1830* (Washington, D. C. 1925), Introduction p. vi. Russell, op. cit., pp. 16-41.
[10]Russell, op. cit., p. 124.
[11]Jeffrey R. Brackett, *The Negro in Maryland* (Baltimore, 1889), p. 33.
[12]Edward Raymond Turner, *The Negro in Pennsylvania* (Washington, 1911), p. 30.
[13]Ibid., p. 124.

women for wives, and are likewise exceedingly impertinent to white people in low circumstances . . . I solemnly swear, I have seen more white women married to, and deluded through the arts of seduction by Negroes in one year in Philadelphia, than for eight years I was visiting (West Indies and the Southern States). I know a black man who seduced a young white girl . . . who soon after married him, and died with a broken heart. On her death he said that he would not disgrace himself to have a Negro wife and acted accordingly, for he soon after married a white woman . . . There are perhaps hundreds of white women thus fascinated by black men in this city, and there are thousands of black children by them at present.[14]

It is difficult to determine to what extent the intermixture of free Negroes and Indians contributed to the growth of the free colored population.[15] There was always considerable association between the Indian and Negro, both in areas given up to Indians and outside of these areas.[16]

Manumission, which was the important means by which the free class was increased, was accomplished through both public and private action. The earliest known will emancipating Negroes is dated 1645. By its provisions a certain Vaughn "freed his negroes at certain ages; some of them he taught to read and make their own clothes. He left them land."[17] As early as 1710 the legislature of Virginia conferred freedom upon a Negro slave for discovering "a conspiracy of divers Negroes for levying war" in the colony.[18] Occasionally, public manumission came as a reward for meritorious public services. For example, Pierre Chastang of Mobile was bought and freed by popular subscription in recognition of public services in the war of 1812 and the yellow fever epidemic in 1819.[19] The philosophy of the Revolution was probably responsible for some of the early fervor in emancipating the slaves.[20] Continued individual manumission in Pennsylvania

[14]Quoted by Carter G. Woodson, in The Beginnings of the Miscegenation of White and Blacks, *The Journal of Negro History*, Vol. III, p. 348.

[15]Carter G. Woodson, *Free Negro Heads of Families in the United States in 1830* (Washington, D. C., 1925), Intro. p. vii. Woodson, The Relations of Negroes and Indians in Massachusetts, *The Journal of Negro History*, Vol. V, pp. 45-52.

[16]Russell, op. cit., pp. 127-130.

[17]*Judicial Cases Concerning American Slavery and the Negro*, edited by Helen T. Catterall (Washington, 1926), Vol. I, p. 59.

[18]Russell, op. cit., p. 43.

[19]Phillips, op. cit., p. 428.

[20]Ibid., p. 425. Russell, op. cit., pp. 54-55. John Daniels, *In Freedom's Birthplace* (Boston, 1914), pp. 7-9.

constantly increased the free class so that slavery became almost
extinct through this means within two generations after 1750.[21]
But private emancipation was not without legal restrictions. In
Virginia private emancipation was forbidden by an act passed in
1723.[22] Owing chiefly to the persistent efforts of the Quakers and
the Methodists, restrictions upon voluntary manumission were
removed in 1782.[23] The subject of restoring the restriction was
warmly debated in the 1804-1805 session of the legislature.[24] In
1806 an act was passed requiring all slaves set free after May 1,
1806, to leave the state.[25] This law caused a large number of
free Negroes to seek asylum in other states.[26] Following closely
upon the Virginia act, Maryland, Kentucky, and Delaware passed
laws prohibiting the entrance of free Negroes, and within twenty-
five years Ohio, Indiana, Illinois, Missouri, North Carolina and
Tennessee passed similar laws or placed rigid requirements upon
the admission of free Negroes.[27]

The first act in Maryland dealing with the manumission of
slaves was passed in 1752. This first act was designed to exercise
some control over masters whose practice of setting their slaves
adrift when they were no longer profitable placed a burden upon
the community.[28] In this same act certain provisions concerning
the form of manumissions and the age and fitness of the slaves
for freedom placed restrictions upon the action of masters. The
desire of individual slave owners and the incessant activities of
the Society of Friends and the Society for the Abolition of Slavery
were constantly in opposition to restrictions upon manumission.[29]
The slave rebellion in Virginia caused the Maryland legislature
to adopt the plan of colonization of the freed Negroes in Africa
as a state policy.[30] According to this act, it was provided that

[21]Turner, op. cit., p. 63. See also Cheeseman A. Herrick, *White Servitude in Pennsylvania* (Philadelphia, 1926), pp. 12-13 and 25-26, for economic causes of the decline of slavery in Pennsylvania.
[22]Russell, op. cit., pp. 52-53.
[23]Ibid., p. 59.
[24]Ibid., p. 67.
[25]Ibid., p. 70.
[26]David Dodge, The Free Negroes of North Carolina, *Atlantic Monthly*, Vol. LVII, p. 23.
[27]Ibid., p. 72.
[28]Brackett, op. cit., p. 149.
[29]Brackett, op. cit., Chap. IV.
[30]Ibid., p. 165.

Negroes already free, who were willing to leave, should be col-
lonized, and that those who were subsequently set free should be
forced to leave the state. There was the important proviso that
annual permits might be granted to deserving freedmen to remain
in the state.[31] Public sentiment failed to enforce the stringent
provisions of this law. Between 1831 and 1845 some twenty-three
hundred and fifty manumissions were reported to the board of
managers, which was empowered to carry out the provisions of
the act of 1831. Of this number eleven hundred were freed out-
right, one hundred and seventy upon the condition, usually, that
they emigrate to Africa; and the remainder after service for a
stated time.[32] Although it is not ascertainable how many freed
slaves received annual permits to remain in the state, the continued residence of a large number of manumitted slaves is an
established fact. In anticipation of the law of 1860, absolutely
prohibiting emancipation, numerous slaves were freed.[33] Whereas
in Maryland in 1830 there were 52,938 free blacks and 102,994
slaves, in 1860 there were 83,942 free blacks and 87,189 slaves.[34]

During the early years of the republic the growth of the free

TABLE I

GROWTH OF THE SLAVE AND FREE NEGRO POPULATION IN THE UNITED STATES:
1790-1860*

CENSUS YEAR	NEGRO POPULATION							
	Total	Free		Slave	Decennial Increase			
		Number	Per Cent		Number		Per Cent	
					Free	Slave	Free	Slave
1860____	4,441,830	488,070	11.0	3,953,760	53,575	749,447	12.3	23.4
1850____	3,638,808	434,495	11.9	3,204,313	48,202	716,958	12.5	28.8
1840____	2,873,648	386,293	13.4	2,487,355	66,604	478,312	20.9	23.8
1830____	2,328,642	319,599	13.7	2,009,043	85,965	471,021	36.8	30.6
1820____	1,771,656	233,634	13.2	1,538,022	47,188	346,660	25.3	29.1
1810____	1,377,808	186,446	13.5	1,191,362	78,011	297,760	71.9	33.3
1800____	1,002,037	108,435	10.8	893,602	48,908	195,921	82.2	28.1
1790____	757,181	59,557	7.9	697,624				

*Negro Population in the United States, 1790-1915, p. 53.

[31]Ibid., pp. 165-166.
[32]Ibid., p. 167.
[33]Ibid., p. 171.
[34]Negro Population in the United States, 1790-1915, Bureau of the Census (Washington, 1918),
p. 57.

Negro population was rapid, amounting to about three times that of the slave population. But after 1810 there was a distinct decline in the rate of increase of the free Negro population, and during the next two decades there was only a small difference in the rate of growth of these two elements in the Negro population. It seems that the increase of 36.8 per cent in the free Negro population in 1830 was probably due to the gradual emancipation which was taking place in northern states.[35] Beginning in 1840, the rate of increase in the slave population was greater than that of the free Negroes, and during the two succeeding decades so far exceeded the rate for the free population that it is difficult to account for the difference.[36]

Although the free Negro population did not grow as rapidly after 1840 as during the preceding decades, there was a steady growth in particular areas. These developments were related in part to certain fundamental changes in the ecological organization of slavery. Phillips has described the changes which had taken place in Virginia and Maryland by 1860.

> Tidewater Virginia and the greater part of Maryland had long been exhausted for plantation purposes and were being reclaimed by farmers working with much the same methods as were followed in the northern states. The large land- and slave-owners mostly followed an example which George Washington had set and divided up their estates into small units, in each of which a few Negroes worked in the raising of varied crops under the control of a white man, who was more a foreman leading the squad than an overseer driving it. Planters who adhered to the old methods were now of decayed estate, supported more by the sale of slaves than by the raising of tobacco. Incidentally, eastern Virginia and Maryland had come to have a very large number of free Negroes.[37]

The relation between these changes and the growth in the free Negro population was probably more than incidental. Free

---

[35]Woodson, *Free Negro Heads of Families in the United States in 1830*, Introduction, p. xviii.

[36]*Negro Population in the United States, 1790-1915*, p. 54. Concerning the decline in the rate of increase of the free Negro population the census report makes the following statement: "Census data do not very clearly account for this decline in the rate of increase of the free element in the Negro population, so far below the rate for the slave population, but it may be noted that, as compared with the slave population, the free colored were somewhat older, and on that account naturally subject to a higher mortality rate, and somewhat less normally distributed by sex and, therefore, probably characterized by a marital condition less favorable to rapid natural increase."

[37]Phillips, *Documentary History of American Industrial Society*, "Plantation and Frontier," Vol. I, Introduction, pp. 88-89.

MAP I.

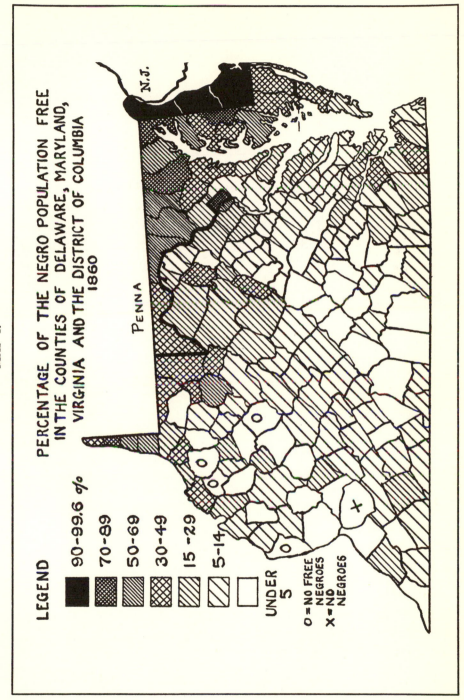

PERCENTAGE OF THE NEGRO POPULATION FREE
IN THE COUNTIES OF DELAWARE, MARYLAND,
VIRGINIA AND THE DISTRICT OF COLUMBIA
1860

LEGEND

90-99.6 %

70-89

50-69

30-49

15-29

5-14

UNDER 5

O = NO FREE NEGROES
X = NO NEGROES

PENNA

N.J.

Negroes did not constitute a conspicuous element in the Negro population where the plantation system existed. The Alabama black lands and the Mississippi and Red River bottoms were still calling for slaves.[38]

Thus we find that the free Negro population was distributed in seven characteristic areas:[39] The Tidewater Region of Virginia and Maryland; the Piedmont Region of North Carolina and Virginia; the Seaboard cities of Charleston, S. C., Mobile, Ala., and New Orleans; the northern cities, including Boston, New York, Chicago, Cincinnati, Philadelphia, Baltimore, and Washington; the Northwest Territory, comprising such settlements as Cass County, Michigan, Hammond County, Indiana, and Wilberforce, Ohio; isolated communities of Negroes mixed with Indians; and, finally, the Seminoles of Florida. In the case of Virginia we find that of the 12,866 free Negroes in 1790 only 75

TABLE II

DISTRIBUTION OF THE FREE NEGRO POPULATION ACCORDING TO STATES IN
1830 AND 1860*

State	1830	1860	State	1830	1860
Maine	1,190	1,327	Georgia	2,486	3,500
New Hampshire	604	494	Alabama	1,572	2,690
Massachusetts	7,048	9,602	Mississippi	519	773
Rhode Island	3,561	3,952	Louisiana	16,710	18,647
Connecticut	8,047	8,627	Tennessee	4,555	7,300
Vermont	881	709	Kentucky	4,917	10,684
New York	44,870	49,005	Ohio	9,568	36,673
New Jersey	18,303	25,318	Indiana	3,628	11,428
Pennsylvania	37,930	56,949	Illinois	1,637	7,628
Delaware	15,855	19,829	Missouri	569	3,572
Maryland	52,938	83,942	Michigan	261	6,799
Virginia	47,348	58,042	Arkansas	141	144
North Carolina	19,543	30,463	Florida	844	932
South Carolina	7,921	9,914	Dist. of Columbia	6,152	11,131
Minnesota		259	Oregon		128
Iowa		1,069	California		4,086
Kansas		189	Texas		355

*Carter G. Woodson, *Free Negro Heads of Families in the United States in 1830*, p. xx; and *Population of the United States in 1860.*

[38]Ibid., pp. 89-90.
[39]From lecture notes on "The Negro in America," by Dr. Robert E. Park.

were in the Trans-Alleghany region, which is now mostly West Virginia; 815 in the Valley district; 3,640 in the Piedmont region and 8,330 in the Tidewater. In 1860 the Tidewater contained 32,841 of the total free Negro population of 58,042.[40] "It appears that Tidewater always had from one-half to two-thirds of the entire free negro class, although after 1830 that section contained less than one-fourth of the white people of the state."[41] In Nasemond County in the Tidewater there were, in 1860, 2,480 free Negroes and 5,481 slaves. Only in one county in the Piedmont did the free Negro population amount to as much as one-sixth of the total Negro population.[42]

In the New England states the free Negro population tended to remain stationary after 1840. In Vermont and New Hampshire there was an actual decline. While the number of free Negroes remained about the same for New York, after 1840 there were gradual increases in New Jersey and Pennsylvania. In the South Atlantic states we find steady growth in the free Negro population, except Florida, where the number remained almost stationary. At the same time the per cent of the total free Negro population in the South Atlantic division declined from 53.8 per cent in 1790 to 44.6 per cent in 1860.[43] During the same period the percentage of free Negroes increased less than one per cent in the North; while in the states of Kentucky, Tennessee, and Alabama there was a significant increase. The growth of the free Negro population in Louisiana showed a distinct decline after 1840. This decline was doubtless due to the stringent laws which were passed in 1830 to restrict the entrance of free Negroes and to restrict the activities of this class. In Mississippi the number of free Negroes was always insignificant. In the Supreme Court of this state it was held that "the laws of this state presume a negro *prima facie* to be a slave." Manumission was limited by a law passed in 1822 to cases in which the slave had performed some meritorious act for the owner or the state, and

[40]Russell, op. cit., p. 13.
[41]Ibid., p. 14.
[42]Ibid., p. 15.
[43]*Negro Population in the United States, 1790-1915*, p. 55.

each proposed emancipation had to be validated by a special act of the legislature.[44] The passage of the Fugitive Slave Law of 1850 was responsible for the flight of many free Negroes into Canada. Those states in the North showing the largest increase in the free Negro population were Ohio, Michigan, and Illinois, states bordering on Canada.[45]

The free Negroes, just as all elements which do not fit into the traditional social order, tended to become concentrated in cities. When the first census was taken in 1790, we find free Negroes in considerable numbers in four cities. According to Russell, "In 1790, when the average ratio of free Negroes to slaves and to whites in the Tidewater section was 1 to 18, in Petersburgh the free Negroes constituted one-fourth of the colored population of the town, and were to the whites as 1 to 4¼. In this town of 3,000 people there were 310 free Negroes."[46] In Virginia in 1850 nearly one-fifth of the total free Negro population lived in towns, while only about one-tenth of the whites lived in urban communities. "In 1860 between a fourth and a third of the whole free colored population lived in towns and cities."[47] A similar situation was to be found in other states. Of the 83,942 free Negroes in Maryland in 1860, 25,680 were in the city of Baltimore.[48] In 1860, 10,689 of the 18,647 free Negroes in the

TABLE III

NUMBER OF SLAVES AND FREE NEGROES IN THE TOTAL POPULATION OF
FOUR LEADING CITIES IN 1790*

| CITY | TOTAL | NEGRO | | | WHITE |
		Total	*Free*	*Slave*	
New York	32,305	3,262	1,078	2,184	29,043
Boston	18,038	761	761		17,277
Philadelphia	28,522	1,630	1,420	210	26,892
Baltimore	13,503	1,578	323	1,255	11,925

*Negro Population in the United States, 1790-1915, p. 55.

[44]Charles S. Snydor, The Free Negro in Mississippi Before the Civil War, *American Historica Review*, XXXII (July, 1927), p. 773.
[45]Woodson, *Free Negro Heads of Families in the United States in 1830*, Introduction, p. xliii.
[46]Russell, op. cit., p. 14.
[47]Ibid., p. 15.
[48]Brackett, op. cit., p. 265.

State of Louisiana lived in New Orleans.[49] More than a third of the free Negro population of Pennsylvania was in Philadelphia in 1860.[50] Concerning Mississippi, Snydor found that "ten per cent of the slaves in Adams County lived in the city of Natchez, 57 per cent of the whites and 73 per cent of the free colored . . . . Vicksburg contained 71 of the 104 free persons of color residing within the county."[51]

---

[49]*Negro Population in the United States, 1790-1915,* pp. 195-96.
[50]Turner, op. cit., p. 253.
[51]Snydor, op. cit., p. 782.

CHAPTER II.

CHARACTER OF THE FREE NEGRO COMMUNITIES

The most striking characteristic of the free Negro communities was the prominence of the mulatto element. About thirty-seven per cent of the free Negroes in the United States in 1850 were classed as mulattoes, while only about a twelfth of the slave population was regarded as of mixed blood.[52] Although no definite information exists concerning the number of mulattoes during the colonial period,[53] we find that in 1752 in Baltimore County, Maryland, 196 of the 312 mulattoes were free, while all of the 4,035 Negroes except eight were slaves.[54] Early in the settlement of Virginia doubt concerning the status of mulatto children was the occasion for special legislation which determined that mulatto children should have the status of their mother.[55] In Maryland, by an act in 1681, children born of white servant women and Negroes were free. By another act in 1692 mulatto children through such unions lost their free status and became servants for a long term.[56] In Pennsylvania the mulattoes followed the status of their mothers, and when the offspring of a free mother became a servant for a term of years.[57]

The conspicuousness of the mulatto element in the free Negro population was not due, therefore, to any legal presumption in its favor. The accessions to the free Negro class through unions of free white women and Negro men, and free colored women

---

[52] "At the censuses of 1850 and 1860 the terms 'black' and 'mulatto' appear not to have been defined. In 1850 enumerators were instructed simply in enumerating colored persons to write 'B' or 'M' in the space on the schedule to indicate black or mulatto, leaving the space blank in the case of whites." *Negro Population in the United States, 1790-1915*, p. 207. See Edward Byron Reuter, *The Mulatto in the United States* (Boston, 1918), p. 116.

[53] Reuter, op. cit., p. 112.

[54] Brackett, op. cit., pp. 175-176.

[55] Russell, op. cit., p. 19.

[56] Brackett, op. cit., p. 33.

[57] Turner, op. cit., pp. 24-25.

and white men was kept at a minimum by the drastic laws against such unions. Nor can the enormous increase in the free mulattoes be accounted for by natural increase from their own numbers. The increase in the number of free mulattoes came chiefly from the offspring of slave women and white masters, who manumitted their mulatto children. Russell says concerning the free mulattoes of Virginia: "The free mulatto class, which numbered 23,500 by 1860, was of course the result of illegal relations of white persons with Negroes; but, excepting those born of mulatto parents, most persons of the free class were not born of free Negro or free white mothers, but of slave mothers, and were set free because of their kinship to their master and owner."[58] Snydor in showing how the sex relations existing between masters and slaves were responsible for the free class in Mississippi, cites the fact that "Of the 773 free persons of color in Mississippi in the year 1860, 601 were of mixed blood, and only 172 were black. Among the slaves this condition was entirely reversed. In this same year there were 400,013 slaves who were classed as blacks and only 36,618 who were mulattoes."[59] In regard to the mulatto character of the free Negro population, it should be noted that the association between the Indians and the Negro was responsible for mulatto communities of free Negroes in Virginia and elsewhere. In Florida the Seminoles were mixed with the Negroes to such an extent that the conflict with the United States was due in part to the attempt of Indian fathers to prevent their Indian-Negro children from being enslaved.[60] There was also considerable interbreeding between the Indians and Negroes in Massachusetts. Many of the offsprings of these relations passed into the colored community as mulattoes.[61] The predominance of the mulattoes among free Negroes was most marked in Louisiana, where 15,158 of the 18,647 free Negroes were mulattoes.[62]

[58]Russell, op. cit., p. 127.

[59]Snydor op. cit., p. 787.

[60]James Johnston, Documentary Evidence of the Relations of Negroes and Indians, *The Journal of Negro History*, Vol. XIV, pp. 38-39.

[61]Woodson, The Relations of Negroes and Indians in Massachusetts, *The Journal of Negro History*, Vol. V, pp. 45-57.

[62]*Population of the United States in 1860*, p. 194.

The free Negroes who were concentrated in urban areas were to a considerable extent able to get some formal education. In 1850 there were large numbers attending schools in northern cities. Boston seemed to have offered the free Negroes the best opportunities for school attendance. In the case of the Virginia cities the absence of any returns for school attendance was due to the stringency of the laws against the instruction of Negroes. The small number attending school in Charleston, S. C. was doubtless attributable to the same cause. Nevertheless, it was a significant fact that the number of adults who could not read or write was almost negligible. The restrictions upon the education of the free Negro population were, probably, as one author holds, never enforced.[63] In New Orleans the large number of Negroes

TABLE IV

SCHOOL ATTENDANCE AND ADULT ILLITERACY AMONG THE FREE NEGRO
POPULATION IN 16 CITIES: 1850*

CITIES	Free Colored Population Total	Number of Free Colored Attending School for County in Which City is Located	Number of Illiterate Adult Free Colored in County
Boston, Mass.(1)** _____	2,038	1,439	205
Providence, R. I._____	1,499	292	55
New Haven, Conn._____	989	360	167
Brooklyn, N. Y._____	2,424	507	788
New York, N. Y.**_____	13,815	1,418	1,667
Philadelphia, Pa._____	10,736	2,176	3,498
Cincinnati, Ohio_____	3,237	291	620
Louisville, Ky._____	1,538	141	567
Baltimore, Md.**_____	25,442	1,453	9,318
Washington, D. C.(2)___	8,158	420	2,674
Richmond, Va._____	2,369	0	1,594
Petersburg, Va._____	2,616	0	1,155
Charleston, S. C.** _____	3,441	68	45
Savannah, Ga._____	686	0	185
Mobile, Ala._____	715	53	12
New Orleans, La._____	9,905	1,008	2,279

*Based on *The Seventh Census of the United States, 1850.*
**Indicates that city and county are coterminous.
(1) Includes Chelsea and North Chelsea.
(2) Statistics are for the city of Washington only.

[63]C. W. Birnie, The Education of the Negro in Charleston, S. C., before the Civil War, *The Journal of Negro History,* Vol. XII, pp. 17-18.

in school was made up of the free mulatto class who constituted a distinct caste in the city. Mobile, Alabama, showed up favorably in regard to the small number of illiterate adults. The absence of returns for school attendance in Savannah reflected the local sentiment against the education of Negroes. This is shown also in the large number of illiterate adults.

The educational status of the free Negroes is an indication of the progress of this class in acquiring the elements of modern civilization. In Charleston, S. C., as early as 1790 the Brown Fellowship Society organized among the free colored people maintained schools for Negro children. Later, other societies were formed especially for the education of indigent and orphaned Negro children.[64] "In New Orleans, where the creoles and freedmen counted early in the nineteenth century as a substantial element in society, persons of color had secured to themselves better facilities of education. The people of this city did not then regard it as a crime for Negroes to acquire an education, their white instructors felt that they were not condescending in teaching them, and children of Caucasian blood raised no objection to attending special and parochial schools accessible to both races. The educational privileges which the colored people there enjoyed, however, were largely paid for by the progressive freedmen themselves. Some of them educated their children in France."[65] At an early period the Negroes of the District of Columbia began to take advantage of the educational opportunities open to them. In 1807 three former slaves built the first colored schoolhouse in the District of Columbia and employed a white teacher. Although this first attempt was not successful, the school was reopened in 1818.[66] The first Negro to teach in the District of Columbia took charge of this school in 1824.[67] Baltimore furnishes another example of early education among the free colored people, and rivals Washington as a city in which

[64]Ibid., p. 15. Woodson, *The Education of the Negro prior to 1861* (New York and London, 1915), p. 129.
[65]Woodson, op. cit., pp. 128-129.
[66]Ibid., p. 131.
[67]Ibid., p. 132.

educational developments represented the efforts of the free colored people themselves. "An adult Negro school in this city had
180 pupils in 1820. There were then in the Baltimore Sunday
schools about 600 Negroes. They had formed themselves into a
Bible association, which had been received into the connection
of the Baltimore Bible Society. In 1825 the Negroes there had a
day and a night school, giving courses in Latin and French. Four
years later there appeared an "African Free School," with an
attendance of from 150 to 175 every Sunday."[68]

Although the colored people of northern cities like New York
and Philadelphia did not support their education to the extent
that they did in Baltimore and Washington, there was a class
of ambitious and thrifty Negroes who paid for the education of
their children.[69] In New England education among the colored
people began almost from the beginning of their enslavement,
but received an impetus after the Revolution.[70] A separate school
for the colored children was established in 1798 with a white
teacher.[71] According to Woodson, who has made a thorough
study of Negro education before the Civil War, "An epoch in the
history of Negro education in New England was marked in 1820,
when the city of Boston opened its first primary school for the
education of colored children."[72]

The social life of the free colored groups centered for the most
part about the churches and the fraternal organizations.[73] In
Boston, as early as 1784, a Masonic lodge was formed with fifteen
members. The first Negro church, originally called the African
Meeting-house, was organized in Boston in 1805.[74] New York,
Philadelphia and Baltimore had large Negro congregations. The
African Baptist Church was organized in Philadelphia in 1809.
Baltimore had ten congregations as early as 1835.[75]   Noah

---

[68]Ibid., pp. 140-141.
[69]Ibid., pp. 144-145.
[70]Ibid., p. 94.
[71]Ibid., p. 95.
[72]Ibid., p. 96.
[73]Woodson, *The History of the Negro Church, 2nd Edition* (Washington, 1921), p. 266. See
Benjamin Brawley, *A Social History of the American Negro* (New York, 1921), pp. 66-74.
[74]Daniels, op. cit., p. 21.
[75]Woodson, *The History of the Negro Church*, p. 136.

Davis, who was allowed considerable freedom by his master in order to find employment that would enable him to purchase his freedom, gives in his autobiography statistics on fifteen Negro churches in 1859 which had a total membership of 6,386.[76] The activity of Richard Allen, who became the first bishop of the African Methodist Episcopal Church, shows how the growing race consciousness of the Negroes in Philadelphia necessitated a separate church in which the Negro could give expression to his own religious life.

> I saw the necessity of erecting a place of worship for the colored people. I proposed it to the most respectable people of color in this city; but here I met with opposition. I had but three colored brethren that united with me in erecting a place of worship—the Rev. Absalom Jones, William White and Dorus Ginnings. These united with me as soon as it became public and known by the elder who was stationed in the city. The Rev. C– B– opposed the plan, and would not submit to any argument we could raise; but he was shortly removed from the charge. The Rev. Mr. W– took the charge, and the Rev. L– G–. Mr. W– was much opposed to an African church, and used very degrading and insulting language to us, to try and prevent us from going on. We all belonged to St. George's Church—Rev. Absalom Jones, William White and Dorus Ginnings. We felt ourselves much cramped; but my dear Lord was with us, and we believed, if it was His will, the work would go on, and that we would be able to succeed in building the house of the Lord. We established prayer meetings and meetings of exhortation, and the Lord blessed our endeavors, and many souls were awakened, but the elder soon forbid us holding any such meetings; but we viewed the forlorn state of our colored brethren, and that they were destitute of a place of worship. They were considered a nuisance.[77]

A similar movement for separate churches among Negroes took place in Washington, D. C., as early as 1820.[78]

The urban environment offered the free Negro an opportunity to enter a variety of occupations which gave him economic security and independence in some cases. In the North he found himself in severe, keen competition with white labor. A study[79]

[76]Noah Davis, *The Narrative of the Life of Noah Davis, a Colored Man, Written by Himself at the Age of Fifty-four* (Baltimore, 1859), p. 85.
[77]Richard Allen, *The Life, Experience and Gospel Labors of the Rt. Richard Allen* (Philadelphia, 1830), pp. 21-28.
[78]John W. Cromwell, The First Negro Churches in Washington, *The Journal of Negro History*, Vol. VII, p. 65.
[79]*A Statistical Inquiry into the Condition of the People of Colour of the City and District of Philadelphia* (Philadelphia, 1849), pp. 17-18.

of the Negro population in Philadelphia in 1847 showed the occupations of 3,358 Negro males to be as follows: mechanics 286; laborers 1,581; seafaring men 240; coachmen, carters, etc. 276; shop keepers and traders 166; waiters, cooks, etc. 557; hairdressers 156; various 96. There were also among the men musicians, preachers, physicians and school teachers. Although the majority of the 4,249 Negro women were classed as washerwomen and domestic servants, 486 were needlewomen and 213 were in trades. The lowest class of colored people who were out of employment found "ragging and boning" a means of livelihood. A significant development in the economic life of the Philadelphia Negro prior to the Civil War was the guild of the caterers which grew up about 1840 and continued until about 1870. The Negro was able to overcome the disastrous competition of foreign labor and find a field where the more energetic among them could achieve economic independence.[80] The free Negroes of Baltimore became formidable competitors of the white laboring population.[81] In spite of the prejudice in New York City against Negro labor, Negroes were engaged in skilled as well as unskilled occupations. In the census for 1850 they were listed chiefly as servants and laborers, but also found places in the skilled occupations as carpenters, musicians, and tailors.[82]

Woodson gives the following picture of the economic condition of the Negroes in Cincinnati.

> Yet undaunted by this persistent opposition, the Negroes of Cincinnati achieved so much during the years between 1835 and 1840 that they deserved to be ranked among the most progressive people of the world. Their friends endeavored to enable them through schools, churches and industries, to embrace every opportunity to rise. These 2,255 Negroes accumulated, largely during this period, $209,000 worth of property, exclusive of personal effects and three churches valued at $19,000. Some of this wealth consisted of land purchased in Ohio and Indiana. Furthermore, in 1839 certain colored men of the city organized "The Iron Chest Company," a real estate firm, which built three brick buildings and rented them to white men. One man, who a few

[80]W. E. Burghardt DuBois, *The Philadelphia Negro* (Philadelphia, 1899), pp. 32-39.
[81]Charles H. Wesley, *Negro Labor in the United States, 1850-1925: A Study in American Economic History* (New York, 1927), p. 32.
[82]Ibid., pp. 37-38

years prior to 1840 had thought it useless to accumulate wealth from which he might be driven away, had changed his mind and purchased $6,000 worth of real estate. Another Negro who had paid $5,000 for himself and family, had bought a home worth $800 or $1,000. A freedman who was a slave until he was twenty-four years old then had two lots worth $10,000, paid a tax of $40, and had 320 acres of land in Mercer County. Another, who was worth only $3,000 in 1836, had seven houses in Cincinnati, 400 acres of land in Indiana, and another tract in the same county. He was worth $12,000 or $15,000. A woman who was a slave until she was thirty was then worth $2,000. She had also come into potential possession of two houses on which a white lawyer had given her a mortgage to secure the payment of $2,000 borrowed from this thrifty woman. Another Negro, who was on the auction block in 1832, had spent $2,600 purchasing himself and family, and had bought two brick houses worth $6,000 and 560 acres of land in Mercer County, said to be worth $2,500.[83]

In the South the free Negroes of Charleston and New Orleans acquired a secure foothold in the economic order. There were listed for 1860 among the taxpayers in Charleston 371 free persons of color, including 13 Indians, who were paying taxes on real estate valued at about a million dollars, and 389 slaves.[84] After the abortive attempt at insurrection by Denmark Vesey in 1822, a memorial was presented to the Senate and House of Representatives concerning the free persons of color. It was argued that this class constituted a menace to white society because their monopoly of the mechanical arts caused German, Swiss and Scotch immigrants to seek homes in the West.[85] In New Orleans, where color was not as great a bar as in many other cities, we find free Negroes in many skilled occupations. Of the occupations given for 1,463 mulattoes in 1850, 299 were carpenters, 143 cigar makers, 213 masons, 76 shoemakers, and 79 tailors. There were listed also 61 clerks, 12 teachers, 1 architect, and 4 capitalists.[86] The property owned by the free colored people in New Orleans in 1860 amounted to about fifteen million dollars.[87] We get some idea of the economic status of the free

---

[83]Woodson, The Negroes of Cincinnati Prior to the Civil War, *The Journal of Negro History*, Vol. I, pp. 9-10.

[84]*List of the Tax Payers of the City of Charleston for 1860*, pp. 315-334.

[85]*Documentary History of American Industrial Society*, "Plantation and Frontier," Vol. II, p. 108.

[86]Wesley, op. cit., pp. 37-38.

[87]Ibid., p. 50.

Negroes in Augusta from an enumeration of the free Negroes in Richmond County, Georgia, in 1819, where there was a total of 194. The occupations recorded for the men were boating, carpentry, harnessmaking, wagoning, and common labor, while the women were engaged in sewing, washing, and domestic service.[88] The above facts give quite a different picture of the economic status of the free colored people from those accounts which represent them as a wholly dependent and debased pariah class.[89] Undoubtedly those observers who have reported miserable conditions of the free Negroes have been faithful in their portrayal of a portion of the free population. But we are primarily interested in the class of free Negroes who were able to achieve some degree of economic independence and culture which became the basis of future progress.

Besides the urban communities which have been described, there were rural communities and isolated communities of Negroes mixed with Indians. We have the following picture of the free Negroes in the rural communities of North Carolina.

> A very few free Negroes prospered, bought larger and better farms, and even owned slaves—one as many as thirty,—which they held up to general emancipation. But generally when they bought land at all the purchase was ludicrously small and, in the country phrase, "so po' it couldn't sprout er pea dout grunt'n." On these infinitesimal bits they built flimsy log huts, travesties in every respect of the rude dwellings of the earliest white settlers. The timber growth being often too scant to afford fence rails, their little patches of phantom corn mixed with pea-vines—or, rather, stubs, their little quota of hulls akimbo on top—were encircled by brush fences, which even by dint of annual renewals were scarcely to be regarded by a beast of average hunger and enterprise.[90]

Dodge's account of the free Negro in the rural sections of North Carolina was descriptive of those in the Piedmont region. In the coastal regions the free Negro was undoubtedly better off.

Turning now to the free Negro communities in the Northwest Territory, we find the settlement in Cass County, Michigan, of

---

[88]*Documentary History of American Industrial Society*, "Plantation and Frontier," Vol. I, pp. 143-47.

[89]See (*H. B. Schoolcraft*) *By a Southern Lady, Letters on the Condition of the African Race, in the United States* (Philadelphia, 1852).

[90]Dodge, The Free Negroes of North Carolina, *The Atlantic Monthly*, Vol. LVII, p. 24.

considerable interest. In this county in 1850 there were 389 colored persons, 19 of whom were attending school; while in 1860 the number had grown to 1,368, among whom there were 981 mulattoes. Concerning the history of this colony one of its descendants gives the following incidents:

> In 1847, a white Virginian named Saunders becoming convinced that slavery was wrong, set his coloured people free, and brought them out to Michigan. In "Chain Lake Settlement" he bought a splendid tract of land nearly one mile square, gave all his people homes, and spent his remaining years among them. Other masters in Virginia, Kentucky, and Tennessee also freed all or a part of their slaves, sometimes the old and infirm ones; sometimes the incorrigibles. These, with free Negroes from Ohio, Indiana and Illinois, continued to swell the population of the Settlement. Most of these people had helped to make the fortunes of their former masters. Now they were eager to accumulate something for themselves and their posterity.[91]

The colony of Negroes at Wilberforce, Ohio, originated largely from the mulatto children of white planters who used to visit the summer resort at Tawawa Springs. The school which was established for these children was first taught by Yankees. According to a woman who went to school there, the planters lavished money on their mulatto children, for whom money was deposited in the banks of Cincinnati.[92] The Randolph slaves, numbering 385, were liberated by the will of John Randolph of Virginia, and settled in Ohio. Their settlement, in Mercer County, was opposed by the whites, and they were compelled to move to a camp near the towns of Piqua and Troy. It seems that they never obtained possession of any of the land which was supposed to have been purchased for them.[93]

[91]James D. Corruthers, *In Spite of Handicap, An Autobiography* (New York, 1916), pp. 17-18.
[92]Concerning the Origin of Wilberforce, *The Journal of Negro History*, Vol. VIII, pp. 335-337.
[93]Letter to Dr. Robert E. Park from an investigator in Ohio seeking information concerning the Randolph slaves, *The Journal of Negro History*, Vol. VII, pp. 207-21⁻. The following news item concerning the Randolph slaves is from the New Orleans (La.) Commercial Times, July 10, 1846:
> "MANUMITTED SLAVES. Three hundred and eighty-five manumitted slaves, freed by the will of the late John Randolph, of Roanoke, passed through Cincinnati, on the 1st instance, on their way to Mercer County, Ohio, where a large tract of land is provided for their future homes. The Times, of that city, understands that the law of that State, known as the Black Law, requiring every colored person coming into the country to give security not to become a public charge, will be rigidly put in force in this instance. Judging from the proceedings of a late public meeting in Mercer County, we imagine this to be true." *Documentary History of American Industrial Society*, "Plantation and Frontier," Vol. II, p. 143.
One of the descendants told the writer recently that they had been unsuccessful in their latest attempt to recover title to this land.

The Pamunky tribe of Indians in Virginia furnishes an illus-
tration of the free communities of Negroes mixed with Indians.
Because of the great infusion of Negro blood in this tribe, it was
claimed by the white citizens of King William County in a petition presented to the State Legislature in 1843 that

> The object of the colonial assembly was to protect a few harmless
> and tributary Indians, but the law which was passed to secure the
> Indians from intrusion on the part of the same white inhabitants has
> unwittingly imposed upon the posterity of the same white inhabitants
> a great grievance, in the presence of two unincorporated bodies of free
> mulattoes in the midst of a large slaveholding community. A greater
> grievance of such character cannot be well conceived, when it is known
> that a large number of free Negroes and mulattoes now enjoy under a
> law enacted for a praiseworthy purpose peculiar and exclusive privi-
> leges such as an entire exemption from taxation, holding land without
> liability for debt, and the land so held properly speaking public land
> belonging to the Commonwealth. . . . The claim of the Indians no
> longer exists. . . . His blood has so largely mingled with that of the Negro
> race as to have obliterated all striking features of Indian extraction.[94]

An isolated community of white, Negro and Indian mixture
has been made the subject of special study by Estabrook and
McDougle.[95] This community originated in the eighteenth century from the descendants of one white man and three Indians.
Later there was an infusion of Negro blood through a few matings
with slaves and Negroes who were free before the Civil War.
They were early separated from the whites, and race feeling has
caused them to form a distinct social group. At the time this
study was made, the population of this group, which is known
as the Win Tribe, was 658. The history of this group indicates
how similar groups have arisen in several counties in Virginia,
North Carolina, South Carolina, Tennessee, Maryland, and Delaware.[96] Although the backwardness of such groups has been
attributed by the authors to the bad effects of racial mixture,
social isolation is a sufficient explanation; for we find that indi-

[94]*Legislative Petitions, Archives of Virginia, King William County, 1843,* Quoted in J. H. Johnston
Documentary Evidence of the Relations of Negroes and Indians, *The Journal of Negro History,*
Vol. XIV, pp. 29-30.
[95]Arthur H. Estabrook and Ivan H. McDougle, *Mongrel Virginians, The Win Tribe,* (Baltimore,
1926).
[96]Ibid., pp. 182-97.

viduals who have had the advantages of outside contacts have not only shown themselves capable, but in some cases have achieved distinction.

Recently Horace Bond had occasion to give achievement tests to the school children in two similar communities in Alabama.[97] He found in both of these communities traditions of French and Spanish and Indian ancestry. Although Negro blood undoubtedly formed a part of their biological heritage, it is strongly denied by these people, who call themselves Creoles and Cajuns, and are isolated from both whites and Negroes.

Having considered the origin of the free Negro population and its distribution in certain characteristic areas, we are prepared to turn to the story of the families which took root in these communities and developed an institutional character.

[97]Horace Mann Bond, Two Racial Islands in Alabama, *American Journal of Sociology*, Vol. XXXVI, pp. 552-67.

CHAPTER III.

THE FREE NEGRO FAMILY

In 1830 we find the free Negro families, which had largely become concentrated in certain areas, enjoying in the South at least their greatest prosperity. We are indebted to the researches of Dr. Woodson for the names of the heads and the number of persons in these families.[98] This information furnishes a basis for the study of the families in the different communities in which we find free Negroes. A glance at Map II shows that the comparatively small number of free families in Georgia were concentrated in Savannah and Augusta. An enumeration in 1819 of free Negroes in Richmond County, in which Augusta is located, gave the names, ages, and occupations of the 194 free persons of color.[99] Although these persons were not recorded according to families, their names and ages as well as the order in which they appeared enable one to determine to some extent family groups. We have already seen how these persons were employed.[100] In most cases the wife as well as the husband was occupied. Eleven years later the total number of free Negroes had been reduced to 172, and they were recorded in the census for 1830 as members of 32 family groups, an average of 5.3 persons to each family. A striking fact about these thirty-two families was that a woman was the head in twenty cases. The predominance of female heads as well as the decrease in numbers may have been due to the attempted insurrection in 1819. By a comparison of names as well as ages we have been able to identify

[98]Woodson, *Free Negro Heads of Families in the United States in 1830.* In some cases slaves held by the free Negroes were counted as part of the family.

[99]Official register of free persons of color in Richmond County, Ga., 1819, printed in the Augusta (Ga.) Chronicle, March 13, 1819, in *Documentary History of American Industrial Society*, "Plantation and Frontier," Vol. I., pp. 143-47.

[100]Supra., p. 20.

MAP II

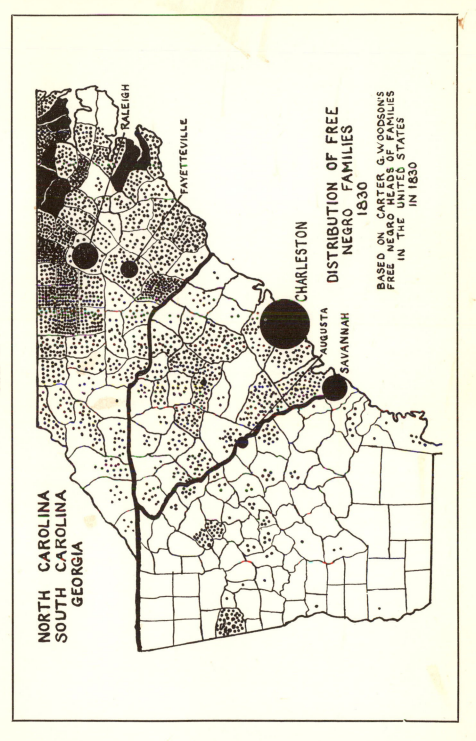

NORTH CAROLINA
SOUTH CAROLINA
GEORGIA

RALEIGH

FAYETTEVILLE

CHARLESTON

AUGUSTA

SAVANNAH

DISTRIBUTION OF FREE
NEGRO FAMILIES
1830

BASED ON CARTER G. WOODSON'S
FREE NEGRO HEADS OF FAMILIES
IN THE UNITED STATES
IN 1830

ten in the list of heads of families in 1830 who were either heads of families in 1819 or children in these families. When we consider the large number of families with female heads in relation to the fact that in 1860 there were 325 mulattoes among the 490 free Negroes enumerated for this county, it does not seem unreasonable to conclude that in many cases white men were the fathers of the children. We know that in one case from such an association which acquired a permanent character came children, one of whom is a distinguished educator whose sisters became teachers and social workers, and whose children are finding a conspicuous place in the Negro world.

Before considering the free Negro families who comprised the comparatively large and prosperous community of free Negroes in Charleston, let us pause to note the history of the descendant of one of the free families scattered in other parts of South Carolina. One of the most distinguished and forceful bishops in the African Methodist Episcopal Church came of a free family residing in Abbeville County. Bishop Turner's biographer gives the following account of the former's ancestry:

> Henry M. Turner was born February 1, 1834, near Newberry, Abbeville, South Carolina, of free parentage. While he was not a slave, he was subject to slave environments. Ownership in himself, only, excepted.
>
> He was the grandson on his mother's side of an African prince, who was brought to this country in the latter part of the Eighteenth Century and held in Slavery, but was soon afterward set free, because South Carolina at that time was a part of a British Colony, and it was contrary to British law to enslave royal blood; hence the freedom of this young Prince was accorded.
>
> David Greer, the illustrious sire of this still more illustrious descendant, not being able to procure passage back to his native country, married a free woman near Abbeville, and planned to make this his home. To this union, aside from many other children, Sarah, his youngest daughter, was born, whom Hardy Turner wooed and wedded. From this union came Henry McNeal Turner, their first born, February 1, 1834.[101]

[101]Henry M. Turner, *Life and Times of Henry M. Turner* (Atlanta, 1917), p. 33. In Woodson's *Free Negro Heads of Families in the U. S. in 1830*, p. 155, there is a David Gryer listed in Abbeville County, South Carolina, as head of a family of six. He is probably a son of the David Greer in the above account of Bishop Turner's grandfather.

Contacts with whites and the kindness of a white woman were responsible for his first knowledge of writing. The law against the instruction of Negroes in South Carolina stopped his education and, although his mother moved to another town and employed a white teacher, a threat of imprisonment again arrested his intellectual development. According to his biographer it was this disappointment that embittered "his mind against the haters of his race, and had much to do with the contempt which he showed in after years for those who opposed the progress of his people."[102]

From what we have already learned concerning the education, economic status, and general culture of the free Negroes of Charleston, it will not be surprising to find a large number of families, which had all the essential characteristics of an "economic-status-child-bearing institution."[103] Probably the wealthiest family among the free Negroes was the Westons.[104] A grandson of this family is reported to be living in Washington, D. C., and is a trustee of the Frederick Douglass Home. Another family, the Holloways, were free people of color under George III. Today a descendant of the family is living in the very house that has been occupied by the family since 1807. It is not without significance as an index to the institutional character of this family, that one of the descendants, who is in charge of one of the largest and best managed Young Women's Christian Associations, still cherishes among her possessions the announcement of her grandmother's golden wedding anniversary reception, which took place in 1885. Although it is impossible to trace the careers of all of the free colored families in Charleston, we shall recount the fate of some of these families and the rôles which others, and especially their descendants, have played in Negro life.

From the lips of a mulatto, the son of a Scotch father and a free mulatto woman, we have learned the histories of some of the families who were listed among the taxpayers of 1860. He was born in Charleston in 1845 and, therefore, knew personally

[102]Turner, op. cit., p. 34.
[103]Ernest Mowrer, *The Family* (Chicago, 1932), p. 260.
[104]Booker T. Washington, *The Story of The Negro* (New York, 1909), Vol. I, p. 206.

many of these people. Some of these families have met the fate of many family lines; they have gradually died out. So far as the Negro group is concerned, this has been the same with quite a number of other families; for they or their descendants went North or to Canada and passed over into the white race. At least seven of these families have disappeared from the Negro group and entered the white race. On the other hand, there are descendants of some of these formerly well-to-do families living in Charleston today whose only heritage is the family name and the traditions of a glorious past.

We shall undertake to catalogue the careers of some of the descendants of these free families. In a southern town we find the grandson of one of the taxpayers of 1860 the principal of the high school. The granddaughter of another is in charge of the girls in a southern college. A distinguished minister in a northern city is the grandson of another taxpayer, who in turn was a descendant of mulatto refugees from Haiti. The granddaughter of another of these free persons of color is the wife of a college president and the leader of the colored women of her state. Descendants of other families listed in 1860 are to be found in the teaching profession, North and South. Likewise, in the cities of the North and South there are social workers, physicians, and ministers, and wives of professional men whose pride in family and social status have come down to them as a heritage from these free families.

A word concerning the descendants, a son and a granddaughter, of Henry Fordham, who was listed among the taxpayers in 1860, will complete our consideration of the Charleston families. His son, James H. Fordham, served in the difficult position of lieutenant of police from 1874 to 1896.[105] During his service he had the respect of his white subordinates and citizens. It has been said that because of the esteem in which he was held by the cultured whites of Charleston, the prejudiced poor whites were prevented from removing him on several occasions. He married into the Weston family, about which we have spoken. A daughter

[105]Theodore D. Jervey, *The Slave Trade, Slavery and Color* (Columbia, S. C., 1925), p. 227.

by this marriage was educated in New England and, after teaching in the South and West, married a physician in a southern town.

In New Orleans and its environment there was, as we have pointed out, a large community of free Negro families similar in some respects to those in Charleston. But, on the whole, the free families in Louisiana inherited traditions different from those of the Negroes and colored people in other parts of the country. The infusion of white blood, which began at a very early date, was due to the association between the Spanish and French settlers and Negro and Indian women. Because of the attitude of the Latins towards racial mixture and the extent to which the mixed bloods became differentiated from the pure Negroes, the mixed bloods came to be recognized as a distinct caste. According to Iberville, the scarcity of white women in Louisiana caused the early Canadian settlers to run "in the woods after Indian girls."[106] For the same reason, apparently, association with Negro women began on a large scale at an early date. Sometime later Paul Alliot, who was seemingly annoyed because mulattoes and Negroes were protected by the government, observed that the wives and daughters of the mixed bloods were "much sought after by white men, and white women at times esteem well built men of color."[107] Perrin du Lac, however, attempted to place the blame chiefly on the Spaniards for the intimacy with the Negroes.

> About one-quarter of the whites are Spaniards, generally from the province of Catalonia. Poor, lazy, and dirty beyond expression, that people mingle indiscriminately with the blacks, free or slave, and are intimate with them in a manner dangerous to the colony. Those blacks, accustomed to be treated as equals or as friends, are most inclined to depart from the respect with which it is so important to inspire them for the whites.[108]

In 1785 the free colored people in Louisiana numbered 1,303.[109] The early sumptuary restrictions on this class were

[106]Arthur W. Calhoun, *A Social History of the American Family* (Cleveland, 1917), Vol. I, p. 331.
[107]*Louisiana Under the Rule of Spain, France, and the United States, 1785-1807* (Cleveland, 1911), Vol. I, p. 71.
[108]Ibid., p. 150, note 4.
[109]Ibid., p. 149.

made untenable when its numbers were augmented by thousands
of fairly well-to-do and cultured mulatto refugees from Haiti,
who settled in New Orleans.[110] By the time of the Louisiana Purchase, this group had become an important enough element in
the population to protest against not participating in a memorial
to Congress concerning the status of the colonists under the new
government.[111] During the defense of New Orleans against the
British in 1814, the free people of color achieved considerable
recognition because of their conduct on that occasion.[112] This
class continued to grow in numbers and in wealth.

By 1830, some of these *gens de couleur* had arrived at such a degree
of wealth as to own cotton and sugar plantations with numerous slaves.
They educated their children, as they had been educated, in France.
Those who chose to remain there attained, many of them, distinction
in scientific and literary circles. In New Orleans they became musicians,
merchants, and money and real estate brokers. The humbler classes
were mechanics; they monopolized the trade of shoemakers, a trade
for which, even to this day, they have a special vocation; they were
barbers, tailors, carpenters, upholsterers. They were notably successful hunters, and supplied the city with game. As tailors, they were
almost exclusively patronized by the élite, so much so that the Le-
goasters', the Dumas', the Clovis', the Lacroix', acquired individually
fortunes of several hundred thousands of dollars. This class was most
respectable; they generally married women of their own status, and led
lives quiet, dignified and worthy, in homes of ease and comfort. A few
who had reached a competency sufficient for it, attempted to settle in
France, where there was no prejudice against their origin; but in more
than one case the experiment was not satisfactory, and they returned
to their former homes in Louisiana. . . .

In fact, the quadroons of Louisiana have always shown a strong
local attachment, although in the state they were subjected to griev-
ances which seemed to them unjust, if not cruel. It is true, they possessed many of the civil and legal rights enjoyed by the whites, as to the
protection of person and property; but they were disqualified from
political rights and social equality. But . . . it is always to be remembered that in their contact with white men they did not assume that
creeping posture of debasement—nor did the whites expect it—which
has more or less been forced upon them in fiction. In fact, their hand-
some, goodnatured faces seem almost incapable of despair. It is true
the whites were superior to them, but they, in their turn, were superior,
and infinitely superior, to the blacks, and had as much objection to
associating with the blacks on terms of equality as any white man

[110]Grace King, *New Orleans, The Place and The People* (New York, 1928), p. 342.
[111]*Louisiana Under the Rule of Spain, France, and the United States, 1785-1807*, Vol. II, p. 279.
[112]George W. Williams, *History of the Negro Race in America* (New York, 1882), Vol. II, pp. 23-27.

could have to associating with them. At the Orleans theatre they attended their mothers, wives, and sisters in the second tier, reserved exclusively for them, and where no white person of either sex would have been permitted to intrude. But they were not admitted to the quadroon balls, and when white gentlemen visited their families it was the accepted etiquette for them never to be present.[113]

Among the free people of color in Louisiana there existed along side of the moral and juridic family a recognized system of concubinage or *plaçage* involving white men and mulatto or quadroon women. A writer reflecting upon these extra-legal family groups has observed that these quadroon women "were, in regard to family purity, domestic peace, and household dignity, the most insidious and the deadliest foes a community ever possessed."[114] On the other hand, a visitor to New Orleans in the '50's, looking at the system more dispassionately, regarded it as "a very peculiar and characteristic result of the prejudices, vices, and customs of the various elements of color, class, and nation, which have been there brought together."[115] In fact, the system of *plaçage* was an accommodation to the legal prescription against intermarriage between white men and these colored women, who were admitted by all observers to be superior generally in grace, beauty, and culture to the white women. At the quadroon balls, to which only white men were admitted, the quadroon women were under the chaperonage of their mothers. The manner in which the men and women became associated in these extra-moral family groups was described by Olmsted as follows:

> When a man makes a declaration of love to a girl of this class she will admit or deny, as the case may be, her happiness in receiving it; but, supposing she is favorably disposed, she will usually refer the applicant to her mother. The mother inquires, like a Countess of Kew, into the circumstances of the suitor; ascertains whether he is able to maintain a family; and, if satisfied with him, in these and other respects, requires from him security that he will support her daughter in a style suitable to the habits she has been bred to, and that, if he should ever leave her, he will give her a certain sum for her future support, and a certain additional sum for each of the children she shall then have.[116]

[113]From unpublished manuscript of Charles Gayarre in Grace King, op. cit., pp. 344-46.
[114]Grace King, op. cit., p. 348.
[115]Frederick Law Olmsted, *A Journey in the Seaboard States in the Year 1853-1854* (New York, 1904), Vol. II, p. 243.
[116]Ibid., p. 244.

The daughters of these quadroon women followed, in some cases, the pattern set by their mothers. Others entered conventional marriages and went to France to live, where their status was not affected by their Negro blood. Since the stigma of Negro blood was always an incentive to become identified with the whites, some passed into the white race by migrating to other sections of the country, or freed their children of the stigma of Negro blood by bribing officials to omit the designation from their baptismal certificates. As New Orleans grew, other mulattoes, taking advantage of the anonymity of the city, passed over into the white race in the city of their birth.

On the other hand, the offspring of these extra-moral associations established conventional families and thereby swelled the number of normal juridic families. Inherited wealth and superior education and culture made them eligible to membership in this class, which was sharply differentiated from the mass of Negroes. The careers of representatives of some of these families have been briefly described by Desdunes, who belonged to this class. There was Paul Trevigne, whose father was a veteran of the War of 1812, who was born in New Orleans in 1825. Desdunes' account continues:

> Trévigne, dans sa jeunesse, a reçu une éducation solide et soignée. Il devint instituteur, occupation qu'il a exercée pendant quarante ans, dans le Troisième District de la Nouvelle-Orléans. Paul Trévigne parlait et écrivait plusiers langues et il était l'ami intime de quelques hommes de haute éducation. Au nombre de ces derniers, on cite Joanni Questy. Basile Crocker, un des plus célèbres maîtres d'armes de notre ville au siècle passé, était aussi dans son intimité. Bien que Trévigne ait formé de bons élèves, aucun d'eux n'a brillé dans la littérature. Cette circonstance est due sans doute à un changement survenu dans les moeurs de la population. Plusieurs de ses élèves ont été officiers dans l'armée de l'Union, ou ils se sont distingués par leur intelligence et leur bravoure.[117]

Another, Eugene Warbourg, who was born in New Orleans about the same year and died in Rome in 1861, was a sculptor.[118] Among the men who succeeded in industry was George Alces, who employed more than two hundred colored creoles in his to-

[117]R. L. Desdunes, *Nos hommes et notre histoire* (Montreal, 1911), p. 90.
[118]Ibid., p. 95.

bacco establishment.[119] Probably one of the best known of these free men of color was Thomy Lafon, for whom a school in New Orleans was named, because of his philanthropies. He distributed his wealth among white and black, Protestant and Catholic. In recognition of his humanitarian interests the state legislature ordered his bust to be set up in one of the public institutions of the city.[120]

The Civil War and Emancipation, and the consequent industrial and social changes, caused the disruption of this class. Many of the free colored people having been slaveholders, were naturally sympathetic towards the Confederacy, and in some cases participated on its side. A review of Confederate troops held in New Orleans in 1861 included a regiment of 1,400 free colored men.[121] There was no community of interest between them and the newly emancipated slaves. Some of them acquired positions of influence during the Reconstruction Period. One of them, Antoine Dubuclet, was state treasurer from 1868 to 1879.[122] When white domination was once more established, the color line was drawn so as to include the former free people of color and their descendants and the ex-slaves in the same category, and subjected both to the same restrictions. Although this brought about some solidarity of interest and feeling, many of the descendants of the free colored caste withdrew to themselves, refusing even to send their children to schools with the Negroes of slave ancestry. Describing the broken morale of this group, Desdunes writes:

> Certains Créoles, de nos jours, sont réduits à ce point de défaillance morale qu'ils méconnaissent et repoussent leurs semblables, leurs parents mêmes.
> Ceux-là aussi, loin de songer à des moyens de délivrance, cèdent à leur faiblesse, sans pouvoir déterminer des principes à suivre ou fixer

[119]Ibid., p. 123.

[120]Grace King, op. cit., p. 353. See also Desdunes, op. cit., p. 123 and *The Journal of Negro History*, Vol. VII, pp. 220-21.

[121]*Negro Year Book*, 1931-1932, p. 329.

[122]Desdunes, op. cit., p. 103. This author writes: "L'injustice du préjugé n'a jamais été plus manifeste que dans l'attitude du public louisianais â l'égard de l'honorable Antoine Dubuclet, trésorier d'Etat de 1868 a 1879. Pendant toute cette époque orageuse, M. Dubuclet a dirigé les finances de la Louisiane, et après ses onze ans de service, il s'est retiré sans laisser derrière lui le moindre vestige de mécontentement ou d'erreur."

une résolution à prendre, comme s'ils voulaient habituer leur nature à la soumission absolue ou à l'oubli de leur individualité. Ils vivent dans un affaissement moral qui semble être le dernier degré de l'impuissance.

Dans cet état de détérioration, ils sont non seulement peu soucieux de relever leur dignité abaissée, mais ils augmentent la somme de leurs erreurs, comme pour multiplier le nombre de leurs supplices. Cependant, il n'est pas difficile de comprendre que, quand l'erreur s'est emparée des esprits, quand l'irrésolution a ramolli les coeurs, l'espérance est bien près d'avoir perdu ses plus fermes appuis.[123]

Some members of the free colored caste and their descendants intermarried with the freedmen, especially those who have become the leaders among the colored people. In such cases they have become a part of the Negro community. We shall conclude our account of the free colored families in New Orleans by tracing the career of one of these families which became integrated into Negro life as we find it today in America.

This family originated on one side with a white merchant who took as his *placée*[124] the daughter of a slave and an Englishman who was the owner of a large plantation. This Englishman was the father also of two other children by another slave woman. One of these, a girl, married an Englishman, and had a daughter who in turn married a German. The issue of this last marriage, a son, went into the white race. When the English plantation owner, who had had the three children by the two slave women, died, his estate was divided between his two surviving daughters. The white merchant and his *placée*, one of these daughters, had four boys and a girl. Our informant, the daughter of one of these boys, spoke as follows concerning her grandmother:

> Grandma was a very beautiful mulattress. She lived very quietly and peacefully with her "mari." It was customary at that time and the custom still lingers among some that: "Un bon plaçage est mieux qu' un mauvais mariage." Grandma was given two slave girls by her father upon her plaçage with (the white merchant). She belonged to the Catholic church and spent her time looking after her children and her "mari."[125]

[123]Desdunes, op. cit., p. 25.
[124]This was the term applied to the free colored women who formed the type of union with white men, which we have described above. See Olmsted, op. cit., p. 245.
[125]*Manuscript document.*

When the merchant's *placée* died, her estate, including what he had inherited from her father, the English plantation owner, was divided among their five children. Their daughter was given a home and the boys divided the income from the rents. One boy, who became a policeman in New Orleans, was noted for his bravery; another was for awhile a government employee and later became the manager of a business concern, while the youngest followed his trade as a shoemaker. They all married into the mulatto families and left their children in good circumstances. These latter have continued to marry into their class, and their children, the great grandchildren of the *placée* of the merchant, are now in the schools of New Orleans. The sister of the four brothers married a tobacco manufacturer who was a descendant of one of the old free colored families. From this union there were five children—three girls and two boys—who have married and moved north, where their children are in school.

Let us return now to the career of the white merchant's fourth son. His daughter, whose testimony concerning her grandmother we have quoted, gave the following facts about her father:

> My father was reared by his grandfather until the latter died. His grandfather had tutors for him and my aunt. He was taught horseback riding and everything related to a life of culture. Upon the death of his grandfather he went back to his father and mother and went to public school. He was about eleven years old at this time. He remained in public school until the age of sixteen. His father, who had a clothing store, thought that he was old enough to come out of school and work in his store.[126]

When twenty years of age he married the daughter of a prosperous mulatto butcher, who was killed by a Negro slave whom he had mistreated. The butcher's wife had had a strange career. She did not know much of her origin except that she was of free origin, because she had been separated from the rest of her family, owing to her brown skin, which contrasted unfavorably with that of her blonde relatives. When we consider the traditions of this woman and her conception of herself, we will understand why she objected strenuously to her daughter's marrying the descendant of slaves. Our informant continues:

[126] *Manuscript document.*

Upon the death of my grandfather (the butcher who was killed by his slave), my grandmother married an independent tobacco manufacturer. There were twelve children of this second marriage. He and grandma, of whom I have a picture, appear to be white. He looks like an old Confederate soldier. Grandma, when a widow, had refused to marry a man who had fought in the Union Army. She regarded him as responsible for losing her slaves. She consistently refused to salute the American flag. Once when she had to get a passport to go to New Orleans and was ordered to salute the American flag, she spat upon it and put it under her feet. She was not punished for this, either because she was a woman or because she was a beautiful woman. Until her death she regarded Abraham Lincoln as her enemy. Grandma strenuously objected to my father's marrying her daughter because my father was a descendant of slaves. All of her children who are living are now in the white race.[127]

Our informant was the second of five children—four of whom survived—by this marriage. She has given us some facts about her early education which were typical of the education of this class.

For neighbors we had on one side Germans and on the other side Irish. The Irish girls were our housegirl and my nurse. The daughter in the German family became my teacher of piano and singing. From the time of my birth my aunt was taught the piano by a French professor. As early as I can remember I used to sit at our piano and play pieces from the Opera by ear, and sing. Later I had an opera troupe of my own composed of my cousins and brothers. We would go through the entire scene of the opera, acting and singing to our best ability.[128]

When she gives an account of her later education we see how the traditions of the free colored caste conflicted with those of the masses of Negroes, and how the community of interest between her father and these masses tended to break down the existing barriers. In fact, she relates later concerning her position in her father's business: "It took me one year to learn how to adapt myself to the situation which required me to show deference and sympathy for Negroes for whose ways I had never had much sympathy or respect."

When I was about eleven years old, I completed what was known as my spiritual education. I had gone to a private school, where I was taught French, English, and the catechism. I had received my first Holy Communion and been confirmed. This meant that I could either

[127]*Manuscript document.*
[128]Ibid.

continue in a convent or get a higher education. At this time my father stepped in and insisted that I attend a colored school because all of his interests were with colored people. My mother objected most strenuously, for she never considered herself a colored woman. But father finally won, and gave me my choice of the state school or a private college.[129]

After our informant's marriage to a mail clerk, which did not turn out well, she became a tutor in a wealthy colored family of free origin that would not send its children to a Negro school. Later she became associated with her father in his business and political career. In both of these fields he achieved distinction, and his daughter became an important factor in the political aspirations of Negro women in the North and South.

The free colored families in Florida resembled those in Louisiana in that the latter also showed the influence of Latin culture. At one time 150 colored soldiers formed part of the garrison of Pensacola.[130] Many of the free colored people were the offspring of Spanish officers and Negro or mulatto women. An investigator found that one of the most prominent colored families in Pensacola traced descent through two Spanish officers.[131] There were evidently a few free Negroes of unmixed blood as, for example, a contractor of free ancestry in Tallahassee, who was apparently of pure Negro blood. Many of the mulatto children, as was the case with the children of Vidal, the Spanish auditor, who died in 1806, inherited their father's property. The following information given us by one writer concerning one of the most prominent free families in Florida gives us some indication of the character of these families.

> Several free colored people at St. Augustine received Spanish grants of land or inherited them from their white forebears. At least one, Joe Sanchez, was a slaveholder at the time of the American occupation, as the archives at St. Augustine will show. One of the most prominent free colored families was that of the Clarkes. Their white father was some time Spanish consul at St. Mary's. He sent his children north to be educated, and two of his daughters married physicians there. They afterwards came back to St. Augustine and tried to secure recognition,

[129]Ibid.

[130]Thomas, David Y., The Free Negro in Florida Before 1865, *The South Atlantic Quarterly*, Vol. X, p. 335.

[131]Ibid., p. 336.

but were unsuccessful, though highly respected by the whites as colored people. One old resident thought that they were given the choice of coming under the patrol law or leaving the country. They chose the latter and went to Nassau. After the war some of them came back and tried to recover some of their property, consisting of real estate and claims on the United States, but they were swindled out of it by rascally agents.[132]

After Florida became a part of the United States, hostility towards the growth of the free colored population was expressed in all kinds of restrictions upon this class. For example, in 1848 all free Negroes were required to have guardians.[133] Therefore, it is not surprising that in 1830 there were only 101 free colored families in the entire state,[134] and in 1860 the total free population had not grown to more than 932.

Most of the free Negro families in North Carolina, as one may see from Map II, were located in the Piedmont and Coastal regions. In North Carolina, as in other states, the free families were found in considerable numbers in the towns and cities. In Fayetteville, in 1830, there were eighty of these families. It was in this city that Henry Evans, a full-blooded free Negro, planted Methodism. Bassett says concerning his activities:

> More striking, but not so typical, is the story of the planting of Methodism in Fayetteville. Late in the eighteenth century, Fayetteville had but one church organization, the Presbyterian, and that had no building. One day there arrived in town Henry Evans, a full-blooded free Negro from Virginia, who was moving to Charleston, S. C., where he proposed to follow the trade of shoemaking. He was perhaps free born; he was a Methodist and a licensed local preacher. ... Some prominent whites, most of whom were women, became interested in his cause. They attended his meetings, and through their influence public opinion was reversed. Then a rude frame building was erected within the town limits, and a number of seats were reserved for the whites, some of whom became regular attendants at his services. The preacher's reputation spread. The white portion of the congregation increased till the Negroes were crowded out of their seats. Then the boards were knocked from the sides of the house and sheds were built on either hand, and in these the blacks were seated. By this time the congregation, which had been unconnectional at first, had been taken into the regular Methodist connection and a regular white

[132]Ibid., p. 337. In 1830 there were four Clarke families in St. Augustine. Woodson, *Free Negro Heads of Families in the United States in 1830*, p. 21.
[133]Thomas, op. cit., p. 343.
[134]Woodson, op. cit., p. 21.

preacher had been sent to it. But the heroic founder was not displaced. A room was built for him in the rear of the pulpit, and there he lived till his death in 1810.[135]

Charles W. Chestnutt, the distinguished Negro novelist, who is now living in Cleveland, is descended from one of these free families.[136] Booker Washington relates the story of another free family. From Mr. Chestnutt he learned that

> a coloured man by the name of Matthew Leary is still remembered in Fayetteville, who, before the war, was the owner of considerable land, a number of slaves, a brick store in the business part of the town, and a handsome residence in a good neighborhood. His sons gained some prominence in North Carolina during the Reconstruction era. Matthew Leary, Jr., went into politics and afterward became a clerk in one of the Government offices in Washington. A younger brother, Hon. John S. Leary, was the first coloured man in North Carolina to be admitted to the bar, of which he remained a respected member until he died at Charlotte, N. C. He was, I understand, at one time a member of the North Carolina Legislature.[137]

Washington has also given us an account of another free family in North Carolina, whose descendants are at present in educational work.

> Another of the successful free coloured people of North Carolina was James D. Sampson, who began life as a house carpenter and became, in the course of time, a man of considerable wealth and some local distinction. I have been informed that one time the Legislature passed a bill granting his family special privileges which were not permitted to other free people of colour. His children, John, Benjamin, and Joseph, were all educated in the North. Benjamin graduated from Oberlin College, and afterward became a teacher at Wilberforce, Ohio. John P. Sampson published at Cincinnati, during the war, the *Coloured Citizen.* After the war he was commissioned by General Howard to look after the coloured schools established by the Freedmen's Bureau in the Third District of North Carolina. He was elected treasurer and assessor of Wilmington, and was candidate for Congress, but was defeated because of the fact, it is said, that his father had been the owner of slaves before the war. While it was true that James D. Sampson owned a number of slaves, it is said that many, if not all, of them were held in trust in order to secure them practical freedom. Recently, George M. Sampson, a grandson of James D. Sampson, visited Tuskegee. He is now a teacher in the State Normal School at Tallahassee, Florida.[138]

[135]John Spencer Bassett, *Slavery in the State of North Carolina* (Baltimore, 1899), pp. 57-58.
[136]Washington, op. cit., p. 203.
[137]Ibid., pp. 203-4. There was a Matthew Leary, returned as the head of a family of seve n, in the census for 1830. Woodson, op. cit., p. 114.
[138]Ibid., op. cit., pp. 204-5.

Although we are not able to trace the descendants of another free Negro who achieved distinction before Emancipation, we include an account of his career, because it indicates how great was the consideration shown members of the free class, who achieved wealth and education, before the triumph of the pro-slavery sentiment. This man was John Chavis.

He was, probably, born in Granville County, near Oxford, about 1763. He was a full-blooded Negro of dark brown color. He was born free. In early life he attracted the attention of the whites, and he was sent to Princeton College, to see if a Negro would take a collegiate education. He was a private pupil under the famous Dr. Witherspoon, and his ready acquisition of knowledge soon convinced his friends that the experiment would issue favorably. After leaving Princeton he went to Virginia, sent thither, no doubt, to preach to the Negroes. In 1801 he was at the Hanover (Virginia) Presbytery, "riding as a missionary under the direction of the General Assembly." In 1805, at the suggestion of Rev. Henry Patillo, of North Carolina, he returned to his native State. For some cause, I know not what, it was not till 1809 that he was received as a licentiate by the Orange Presbytery. Although he preached frequently to the regular congregations at Nutbush, Shiloh, Island Creek, and other churches in the neighborhood, I do not find that he was called to a church as pastor. Mr. George Wortham, a lawyer of Granville County, said in 1883: "I have heard him read and explain the Scriptures to my father's family repeatedly. His English was remarkably pure, containing no 'negroisms;' his manner was impressive, his explanations clear and concise, and his views, as I then thought and still think, entirely orthodox. He was said to have been an acceptable preacher, his sermons abounding in strong common sense views and happy illustrations, without any efforts at oratory or sensational appeals to the passions of his hearers. He had certainly read God's Word much and meditated deeply on it. He had a small but select library of theological works, in which were to be found the works of Flavel, Buxton, Boston, and others. I have now two volumes of 'Dwight's Theology,' which were formerly in his possession. He was said by his old pupils to have been a good Latin and a fair Greek scholar. He was a man of intelligence on general subjects and conversed well." He continued to preach, till in 1831 the Legislature forbade Negroes to preach. It was a trial to him, and he appealed to the Presbytery. That body could do nothing more than recommend him "to acquiesce in the decision of the Legislature referred to, until God in his providence shall open to him a path of duty in regard to the exercise of his ministry." Acquiesce he did. He died in 1838, and the Presbytery continued to his widow the pension which it had formerly allowed to him.

Mr. Chavis' most important work was educational. Shortly after his return to North Carolina he opened a classical school, teaching in Granville, Wake, and Chatham Counties. His school was for the patronage of the whites. Among his patrons were the best people of the neighborhood. Among his pupils were Willie P. Mangum, afterwards United States Senator, and Priestly Mangum, his brother, Archibald and John Henderson, sons of Chief Justice Henderson, Charles Manly, afterwards Governor of the State, Dr. James L. Wortham of Oxford, N. C., and many more excellent men who did not become so distinguished in their communities. Rev. James H. Horner, one of the best teachers of high schools the State has produced, said of John Chavis: "My father not only went to school to him but boarded in his family. . . . The school was the best at that time to be found in the State."[139]

In 1830 John Chavis was teaching a school for free colored people in Raleigh, where Lunsford Lane, of whom we shall now give an account, succeeded in purchasing himself and family and acquired property. Lunsford Lane was born a slave in Raleigh in 1803. His mother was a house servant in the family of a plantation owner, while his father was owned by a neighbor. Of his early childhood he wrote:

> My early boyhood (was spent) in playing with the other boys and girls, colored and white, in the yard, and occasionally doing such little matters of labor as one of so young years could. I knew no difference between myself and the white children; nor did they seem to know any in turn. Sometimes my master would come out and give a biscuit to me, and another to one of his own white boys; but I did not perceive the difference between us. I had no brothers or sisters, but there were other colored families living in the same kitchen, and the children playing in the same yard, with me and my mother.[140]

He became conscious of his slave status when he began to work. He said:

> They began to order me about, and were told to do so by my master and mistress. I found, too, that they had learned to read, while I was not permitted to have a book in my hand. To be in the possession of anything written or printed was regarded as an offence. And then there was the fear that I might be sold away from those who were dear to me, and conveyed to the far South. I had learned that being a slave I was subject to this worst (to us) of all calamities; and I knew of others in similar situations to myself, thus sold away. My friends were not numerous; but in proportion as they were few they were dear; and the thought that I might be separated from them forever was like that of having the heart torn from its socket; while the idea of being conveyed to the far South seemed infinitely worse than the terrors of death.

[139]Bassett, op. cit., pp. 73-75.
[140]Lunsford Lane, *The Narrative of Lunsford Lane, Formerly of Raleigh, N. C.* (Boston, 1842), pp. 5-6.

To know, also, that I was never to consult my own will, but was, while
I lived, to be entirely under the control of another, was another state
of mind hard for me to bear. Indeed, all things now made me feel,
what I had before known only in words, that I was a slave. Deep was
this feeling, and it preyed upon my heart like a never dying worm. I
saw no prospect that my condition would ever be changed. Yet I
used to plan in my mind from day to day, and from night to night,
how I might be free.[141]

Lunsford Lane has also given us an account of his first efforts
to buy his freedom.

One day, while I was in this state of mind, my father gave me a
small basket of peaches. I sold them for thirty cents, which was the
first money I ever had in my life. Afterwards I won some marbles and
sold them for sixty cents, and some weeks after Mr. Hog from Fayetteville came to visit my master, and on leaving gave me one dollar.
After that Mr. Bennahan from Orange county gave me a dollar, and a
son of my master fifty cents. These sums, and the hope that then
entered my mind of purchasing at some future time my freedom, made
me long for money, and plans for money-making took the principal
possession of my thoughts. At night I would steal away with my axe,
get a load of wood to cut for twenty-five cents, and the next morning
hardly escape a whipping for the offence. But I persevered until I had
obtained twenty dollars. Now I began to think seriously of becoming
able to buy myself; and cheered by this hope, I went on from one thing
to another, laboring "at dead of night," after the long weary day's
toil for my master was over, till I found I had collected one hundred
dollars. This sum I kept hid, first in one place and then in another, as
I dare not put it out, for fear I should lose it. . . .
    After this I lit upon a plan which proved of great advantage to me.
My father suggested a mode of preparing smoking tobacco, different
from any then or since employed. It had the double advantage of giving
the tobacco a peculiarly pleasant flavor, and of enabling me to manufacture a good article out of a very indifferent material. I improved
somewhat upon his suggestion, and commenced the manufacture,
doing, as I have before said, all my work in the night. The tobacco I
put up in papers of about a quarter of a pound each, and sold them at
fifteen cents. But the tobacco could not be smoked without a pipe, and,
as I had given the former the flavor peculiarly grateful, it occurred
to me that I might so construct a pipe as to cool the smoke in passing
through it, and thus meet the wishes of those who are more fond of
smoke than heat. This I effected by means of a reed, which grows
plentifully in that region; I made a passage through the reed with a hot
wire, polished it, and attached a clay pipe to the end, so that the smoke
should be cooled in flowing through the stem, like whiskey or rum in
passing from the boiler through the worm of the still. These pipes I sold
at ten cents apiece. In the early part of the night I would sell my tobacco and pipes, and manufacture them in the latter part. As the Leg-

[141]Lane, op. cit., pp. 7-8.

islature sit in Raleigh every year, I sold these articles considerably to the members, so that I became known not only in the city but in many parts of the State as a tobacconist.[142]

When Lunsford Lane was twenty-five he married, according to the usual slave ceremony, a slave woman. Within two years his savings had been consumed because he was forced to support his two children and his wife, whose master would not contribute to their upkeep. Fortunate for Lane, the death of his master required his mistress to sell some of the slaves and to hire out others, in order to settle the indebtedness against the estate. Lane hired his time at a price varying from one hundred to one hundred and twenty dollars a year. Then he began the manufacture of pipes and tobacco on a large scale. His business acumen and his ambition to earn enough to obtain his freedom are shown in the following account which he gives of his activities.

> I opened a regular place of business, labelled my tobacco in a conspicuous manner with the names of "Edward and Lunsford Lane," and of some of the persons who sold it for me—established agencies for the sale in various parts of the State, one at Fayetteville, one at Salisbury, one at Chapel Hill, and so on—sold my articles from my place of business, and about town, also deposited them in stores on commission, and thus, after paying my mistress for my time, and rendering such support as necessary to my family, I found in the space of some six or eight years that I had collected the sum of one thousand dollars. During this time I had found it politic to go shabbily dressed and to appear to be very poor, but to pay my mistress for my services promptly. I kept my money hid, never venturing to put out a penny, nor to let anybody but my wife know that I was making any. The thousand dollars was what I supposed my mistress would ask for me, and so I determined now what I would do.[143]

Lane succeeded in purchasing his freedom for $1000 through his wife's master, since he could not legally buy his own freedom. In fact, his wife's master could not manumit him legally, since Lane had not performed, according to the law, any "meritorious service"; therefore it was necessary to take him to New York in order to give his manumission a legal status. Then Lane turned his thoughts to purchasing the freedom of his family, consisting

[142]Lane, op. cit., pp. 8-10.
[143]Ibid., pp. 15-16.

at the time of his wife and six children. At first his wife's master wanted $3,000 for the family, but after some bargaining he let Lane have them for $2,500. He gave five notes of five hundred dollars, each payable the first of January for five years, beginning in 1840. January, 1839, found Lane and his family in their own home, which had already been purchased.

Lunsford Lane's success in business, and especially his freedom, incited the hostility of the white populace. He was charged with violating the law which forbade free Negroes from other states to enter the State of North Carolina, and was ordered to leave the state within twenty days. He appealed to his white friends and through their influence was permitted to remain in the state until the meeting of the legislature. His petition to the legislature to be allowed to remain in the state was voted down. The petitions of two other free colored people were treated in the same manner. On the eighteenth of May, 1841, Lane, having paid for one of his daughters, set out for New York.

About a year later, when he had sufficient money to pay for the remainder of his family, he sought permission from the governor to re-enter the state in order to conclude the transaction. Although the governor denied having authority to grant this permission, he informed Lane's white friends that it would be safe for him to come quietly and leave as soon as possible. In fact, one white friend implied in a letter that the time was propitious, because the people were "alive . . . . on the subjects of temperance and religion."[144] This, however, did not prevent his arrest on the unfounded charge of having delivered abolition speeches in Massachusetts. He was ordered out of the city, but a mob made it necessary to place him in a jail for safe keeping. Upon his release he was tarred and feathered by a mob of working men, who were satisfied with inflicting some form of humiliation. After he had settled for his family and was prepared to leave, his mother's mistress, affected by the separation of Lane from his mother, permitted her to accompany the family.

During the autumn of 1897 Bassett by chance noticed at a

[144]Ibid., pp. 35-36.

Negro fair in North Carolina a placard which read: "Horses
Owned and Exhibited by Lunsford Lane." Approaching a Negro
farmer, he asked: "Who is Lunsford Lane?" "I am, sir," was
the reply. "What kin are you to the original Lunsford Lane?"
"Don't exactly know, sir; reckon he was my uncle." "What became of him?" questioned Bassett, in order to draw him out. The
man answered: "Think he must 'a' emigrated." Bassett concludes
his account with the observation:

> Here was thrift enough to become the owner of a pair of very good
> farm horses, but not enough of intelligence to remember the fate of the
> most remarkable member of the man's family, who was still alive
> thirty years ago. How much did that family lose in the emigration of
> Lunsford Lane![145]

The town of Newbern also had its community of free colored
families, that numbered 104 in 1830. Bassett has furnished a
description of some of the free Negroes in Newbern before the
Civil War.

> John C. Stanley was a mulatto, the son of an African born slave
> woman, who was brought to Newbern, N. C. (from the West Indies) be-
> fore the Revolutionary War. He was a barber by trade and throughout
> his days of manhood was known as "Barber Jack." He was a faithful
> servant, and in 1808 he was liberated by the General Assembly on
> petition of Mrs. Lydia Stewart, into whose possession he had come.
> He soon began to acquire Negro slaves and land, till at length he had
> sixty-four slaves and as many more bound free Negroes working his
> several plantations. Says Col. John D. Whitford: "He was popular,
> too, with both slave and free Negroes generally, notwithstanding he
> was a hard taskmaster. Yes, he worked all well and fed and clothed
> indifferently." He married a Moor, a copper colored woman who was
> not a slave. He got his start in the barber business—although he made
> much of his money by discounting notes. Certain white men of means
> who did not care to go openly into the business of sharp discounting,
> took him for a partner and furnished the means. He had three sons,

---

[145]Bassett, *Anti-Slavery Leaders of North Carolina* (Baltimore, 1898), p. 74. Speaking of the effect
upon the development of the Negro of the laws which made it impossible for free Negroes of Lane's
type to remain in the South, Bassett says: "The little glimpse that we have of his real self shows
what a promise of hope he was for the race he represented. We know enough to be certain that
it was a most short-sighted policy in his State that drove him and a number of others out of the
community, and made impossible the development of other negroes like unto him. Since the war
we have sadly missed such strong characters in our negro population. Twenty-five years before the
war there were more industrious, ambitious and capable negroes in the South than there were
in 1865. Had the severe laws against emancipation and free negroes not been passed, the coming
of freedom would have found the colored race with a number of superior individuals who in every
locality would have been a core of conservatism for the benefit of both races. Under such conditions Lane would have been of great beneficent influence." Ibid., p. 74.

John, Alexander and Charles. John became an expert bookkeeper and was employed in that capacity by a prominent firm. John C. Stanley amassed a fortune supposed to be worth more than $40,000; but in his old age he lost much of it by bad management. His family held themselves aloof from the other Negroes of the community. They were members of the Presbyterian Church, to which Mrs. Stewart, his former mistress, had belonged. This lady lived till 1822, and when old and feeble, could be seen on the streets in fine weather supported on the arm of her faithful old servant—now fourteen years a free man. Thus she took the air, and thus she went to church on Sunday. When the couple had arrived at the church, John would conduct her to her pew, and then leave her to take his seat with his own family in the place assigned to colored people.

. . . In Newbern, especially, there were a number of such thrifty colored men. Notable among these was John Good. He was a son of his master and for a long time a slave. When the master died, his two surviving children, who were daughters, had but little property besides this boy, John, who was a barber. John took up the task of supporting them. He boarded them in good houses and otherwise provided for them well. His faithfulness won him many friends among the best citizens, and when both of his mistresses were married, these friends united to persuade the owners to liberate him as a reward for his services. Unfortunately, freedom proved no boon. He fell into bad habits, took to drink, and soon died. There were other thrifty and notable free Negroes in the same place, as, for example, John Y. Green, a carpenter and contractor; Richard Hazel, a blacksmith of means; Albert and Freeman Morris, described as two "nice young men" and thoroughly respected, tailors by trade; and Scipio, a slave of Dr. Hughes, who was a blacksmith and owner of a livery stable. Another was Fellow Bragg, a tailor, who was thoroughly conscientious and so good a workman that prominent people were known to move their custom to the shops at which he was employed in order that he might work on it. Most of these men moved to Cincinnati sooner or later.[146]

Fortunately, we have a comprehensive history of one of these free families in Newbern, from which we shall give some of the more significant details. The historian, who is also a member of this family, gives the following account of its origin on his father's side.[147]

John P. Green, the subject of this sketch, was born in the old town of Newberne, North Carolina, on the second day of April, 1845. His parents were John R. Green and Temperance Green, both of whom were free colored people of mixed blood, and highly respected by the people of both races in that community.

[146]Bassett, *Slavery in the State of North Carolina*, pp. 44-45.
[147]In 1929, when Mr. John Patterson Green was almost eighty-five years old, he was still trying jury cases before the Cuyahoga County (Ohio) bar.

John R. Green, the father, was the reputed son of John Stanley (spelled by him Stanly) of North Carolina, who was the son of John Wright Stanley, of the same place, and who, during our Revolutionary War, for a long period of time maintained a fleet of fourteen privateers, in the vicinity of the West India Islands, which preyed upon British Commerce quite successfully until, being attacked in its West Indian harbor of refuge by a portion of the British Navy, it was thoroughly destroyed, and Stanley betook himself to commerce and merchandise, in the old North Carolina town, at that time the capital of the state.

This is the same John Wright Stanley upon whose head, with that of William Gaston, a great Revolutionary patriot of the same state and community, was placed a premium by the British military authorities during that war, and who, in the darkest days of the War of Independence, loaned General Nathaniel Greene the sum of forty thousand pounds, which "I may say, was never repaid to him, and when we consider the scarcity of money at that time, and that forty thousand pounds was as valuable then as two hundred thousand pounds is now, we can form a correct estimate of the patriotism of that 'Son of the Revolution.' "[148]

His father's mother was a woman of African descent who served as a mammy in the family of Governor Speight. The story continues:

Such was the love and affection for Sarah Rice, on the part of the Speight Family that they "set her free," manumitted—emancipated her, giving her, at the same time the sum of two hundred dollars, as required by the law of the State at that time.

Previous to this important event in the life of this favored nurse, she had been delivered of a wee boy baby, whom she had named for herself only,—Johnnie Rice,—not daring to disclose his true paternity; but, subsequently, having attained her freedom, she called him Johnnie Green, for a little boy whom she had nursed; for Johnnie, having been born when his mother was still in the bonds of slavery, followed his mother's slave condition; and, not having been manumitted with her, he was still the slave of the Speight estate; and to let it be known that he was the "natural" son of John Stanley, the fatal ball from whose pistol had killed the Governor, would, in all probability, have sealed his fate adversely.

So Johnnie Green became, in later days, John R. (Rice) Green; and this writer, his son, has flaunted the green flag as John P. (Patterson) Green ever since. Sometimes, really, "fact is stranger than fiction."[149]

The origin of the maternal side of the family is told by the author in the following words:

[148]John P. Green, *Fact Stranger Than Fiction* (Cleveland, 1920), pp. 1-2.
[149]Ibid., pp. 3-4.

My mother, Mrs. Temperance Durden Green, was a quadroon by blood, and was a direct descendant, on both her father's and her mother's side, from those Scottish and Yorkshire Englishmen who followed the flag and fortunes of the last "Pretender" descendant of the unfortunate James II, of England, in 1745; and after having met disastrous defeat at Derby, almost at the gates of London, were expatriated and in large numbers found asylum in North Carolina, notably in the counties of Cumberland and Sampson, where, by thrift and economy, they left a numerous and wealthy progeny, as may be seen by tourists and others today.

In the latter part of the eighteenth century, 1792, to be specific, there resided near the town of Clinton, in Sampson County, North Carolina, about thirty miles from the city (then town) of Fayetteville, in the same state, a family, containing two beautiful daughters, of which a man, Chestnut (or Chestnutt) by name, was the head. This *pater familias* was a well-to-do farmer and, with his wife and daughters, was known and respected, far and wide, by persons of his class; moreover, since his daughters were young and comely, they were frequently favored by the calls of young gentlemen in the vicinage, who, socially and financially, deemed themselves their superiors.

In the course of time the young ladies became greatly enamored of two of these young men; but, since they did not hasten to make to them proposals of marriage, they had recourse to the advice and services of a "likely" young colored man (the slave of their father), who advised them, in the premises, with the result that, ere long, each became the mother of a little colored girl; one of these baby girls was named Obedience, which was transformed to "Bede"; this one was my grandmother, born in the same year as my father, 1793; the child of the other girl, sister of this first mother, was named Alice but, invariably, as long as she lived, called "A-lice."

A glance will suggest that these two babies, being the offspring of one father by two sisters were, at once, sisters and cousins! This condition during the womanhood of these two colored girls was doubly complicated, when each girl presented to two white brothers, severally, a child, one of whom was my mother.[150]

Mr. Green's father, having been born before the emancipation of his mother, inherited the slave status. When he was thirteen he was apprenticed to a tailor and continued at this trade until his death in 1850. During his apprenticeship he managed to save $1000, with which he later purchased his freedom. At the same time he learned to read and write through one of those subterfuges characteristic of the manner in which both the enslaved and free Negro circumvented the obstacles to learning. Mr. Green writes:

[150]Ibid., pp. 5-6.

The method in practice between my "Daddy" and the blind man was as follows: Dad would call the letters of a word, and the blind man would tell him how to pronounce it; and "Jack-the-weazel," like his forebears, being naturally clever, ere long was reading, in the same little book, the monosyllabic sentences, beginning, "No man may put off the law of God."[151]

We get some indication of the status of Mr. Green's father in the community from the following:

In this connection it may not be amiss to state that, although born and reared a slave, and residing in a slave-holding community, my daddy so deported himself as to merit and receive kind and courteous treatment from all. He owned and occupied with his family a pew in Christ Episcopal Church, which was the most wealthy and aristocratic congregation in that part of the state; while the other members, with two exceptions, sat in the galleries; and as proving how tenacious he was of what he conceived to be his rights, it may be stated that, when the Reverend Doctor Buxton (white), a clergyman of the Episcopal Church, married him and my mother in Fayetteville, North Carolina, in 1837, and did not wear his clerical robe, he would not give him a bill which he carried in his vest pocket for him.[152]

When John R. Green died, his son, the historian of the family, was five years of age. The death of his father meant a complete change in the fortunes of the family, and forced the mother to move from her "palatial residence of yore, mahogany furniture, cut-glass, silver service, the ministration of maid servants and hosts of friends, and repairs, with her little brood, to a rude cottage in an obscure section of the old town."[153] The mother undertook the support of herself and the three children through sewing and whatever assistance the children could add.

In 1857, acting upon the advice of a friend to bring her family to "the land of freedom," the mother followed other free colored families and moved to Cleveland. Although Mr. Green had acquired some education through private tutoring from the colored people of Newbern, his formal education began after the family moved to Cleveland. His education was interrupted because of the struggles of the family in the northern city. He

[151]Ibid., p. 12.
[152]Ibid., p. 13. This was a second marriage, the first wife having died the same year. Ibid., p. 13. In Woodson's *Free Negro Heads of Families in the United States in 1830*, p. 113, there is a John R. Green listed as the head of a household of ten for the town of Newbern.
[153]Ibid., p. 22.

succeeded, however, in completing the high school in Cleveland in 1869. Later he completed a law course and was admitted to the bar of South Carolina. After engaging in the politics of that state during the troublous reconstruction period, he returned to Cleveland and continued his career in law as well as in politics. He served in both the General Assembly and Senate of the State of Ohio.

Since our interest is primarily in the origin and progress of these free families before Emancipation, we shall give only a little space to the later career of the family. For example, two of his sons followed him in the law profession. There are now grandchildren who are building upon the foundation laid by their grandfather.

We shall turn now to the story of two free colored families located in a rural community in the northeastern section of the state. One of the youngest representatives of one family is at present a successful physician in New Jersey. The story of his ancestors leads us back to one of those cases concerning which we spoke at the beginning of this essay, of sexual association of free Negroes and white women during the Colonial period and the early days of the Republic. Round the beginning of the nineteenth century a poor white woman, who ran a ferry, had two daughters by a colored man of Negro, Indian, and white blood. One of these girls was married to a full-blooded free Negro carpenter, who, as his seventy-eight year old grandson informed the writer, "wanted a free woman, so that white people could not interfere with his married life." A son from this union acquired land and reared a large family. One of the children, the father of the physician mentioned above, left North Carolina in 1885 and settled in New Jersey, where he gave his children the educational advantages of the North.

The history of the other free family will be traced in greater detail. In 1930, at the reunion of the family, which has taken place for forty years, there were gathered four generations. The granddaughter of the ancestor, whose tomb, with that of his wife, is close to the ancestral home, which has been a part of the family property for a hundred years or more, read a paper in which she recalled the pious and noble character of her grand-father, the traditions of the family, and exhorted the descendants to "walk in the straight path" that he had cut for them. The tomb, to which the family repaired as a part of the ceremony, showed that her grandfather was born in 1814 and died in 1892, while his wife, who was born in 1824, survived him three years. Although the members of the family recall these two ancestors as the founders of the family, there was some knowledge of the former's parents, who were also free.

An old minister who was acquainted with the ancestor who was eulogized, described him as "an old Puritan in his manners and morals, and the only advocate of temperance in the county for years." He was the father of fourteen children, ten of whom —four girls and six boys—reached adulthood. One daughter married a man who was killed in service during the Civil War. The oldest son, one of the first graduates of Hampton Institute, taught school. Among the other boys, who also attended Hampton, were a carpenter, a brickmason, a school principal and the founder of an orphanage. All ten of the children married and have children and grandchildren in different parts of the country. One of the latter, the vice-principal of a high school in a large city, was present at the family reunion in 1930.

If we should trace the family histories of many leaders of the Negro in business, in religion, and in education, as, for example, a professor at Fisk University, they would lead back to free families in North Carolina, who made the first steps in the acquisition of wealth and education, in spite of the restrictions upon their activities.

Having given an account of the free colored families of North Carolina, we shall pass on to those in Virginia. We have seen that in Virginia in 1850 a fifth of the free Negro population was concentrated in urban areas. Space will only permit consideration of the free families of Petersburg, where as far back as 1790 they constituted a fourth of the entire Negro population. In 1830 there were in this city among the 2,032 free Negroes 503 heads of

families, 107 of whom owned slaves.[154] Many of the free families
in Petersburg at this time had enjoyed a regular family life for
several generations.[155]   The history of one of these families is
given as follows by Professor Jackson.

> The first of the Jarratt family of whom we learn is Richard Jarratt,
> who was born in Pocahontas about 1779 and was married in 1803 to
> Betsy Rollins. In 1820 this man is recorded as the owner of a house and
> lot in Pocahontas valued at $831.25, with the extremely low rate of
> taxation on the same at $1.80. In 1828 he further adds to his small
> holdings by buying a lot from one David Cary. This Jarratt ran a boat
> from Petersburg to Norfolk and kept a regular account book of his
> daily cargo. Another indication of the worth of this man is that he had
> his children educated. In 1814 he paid to Joseph Shappard, another
> free Negro, the sum of $2.50 as one month's tuition charge for teaching
> his daughters, Jane and Ellie.
>
> One son of Richard Jarratt was Alexander, who was born in Poca-
> hontas in 1806 and died in 1869. Like the father, he took to the water,
> at one time being a steward on a vessel which ran to New York. Alex-
> ander Jarratt added to the standing of his family by his marriage to
> Nancy Fuller, of Norfolk, who in turn came from a substantial family.
> John Fuller, of Norfolk, and his four sons, all went to Liberia about
> 1855. One of these became a mayor and the others high sheriffs.
>
> For a while Alexander Jarratt and his family lived in Norfolk, where
> they made frequent trips by water to New York on both social and
> business missions. . . . .
>
> There were twelve children born to Alexander and Nancy Jarratt.
> Two of them, John Fuller Jarratt and Mrs. Lavinia Anderson, are still
> living. John, the last of this family to be mentioned, was born about
> 1848. From 1869 to 1898 this Jarratt was employed on the Appomattox
> River. He was in charge of a government tug boat, the *C. B. Phillips*,
> and as captain of the same boat had charge of all of her property while
> in operation. This boat was used for the constant improvement of the
> river by dredging from Petersburg to City Point. At various times he
> served as a watchman and had charge of a warehouse. This man's
> prominence was due to his being regarded by all as an expert in improv-
> ing the channel bed of the river. After a long, useful career, first in the
> capacity mentioned and later as a fisherman, John Fuller Jarratt
> ceased work only eight years ago.[156]

Another family which has had an outstanding career in
Petersburg for six generations is the Colson family. The earliest
ancestor concerning whom we have any historical record was
probably born during the American Revolution in Petersburg.

[154]Luther P. Jackson, Free Negroes of Petersburg, Virginia, *The Journal of Negro History*, Vol.
XII, p. 367.
[155]Ibid., pp. 367-68.
[156]Ibid., pp. 369-71.

Our first real knowledge of him comes in 1804, when, for the sum of forty-five pounds, he purchased from Hector McNeil, a white merchant of Petersburg, "one certain piece or parcel of land situate, lying and being in the town of Petersburg aforesaid, on the east side of the street known and distinguished in the plan of the said town by the name of Union Street." In 1820 this property, consisting of house and lot, was valued at $1,050. In the meantime he had also bought one lot on Oak Street, which was assessed at $131.25. This James Colson becomes the head of a remarkable line of descendants. When he died, in 1825, his property was taken over by his son, William Colson. The son in his early years was a barber in Petersburg, but a few years after his marriage to Sarah Elebeck, in 1826, he emigrated to Liberia in connection with the colonization movement of that time. In Liberia he engaged in a mercantile enterprise with Joseph Jenkins Roberts, who, too, came from Petersburg.[157]

William Colson was the father of three children, William, Mary, and James Major. The last of these particularly comes easily within the memory of Petersburg citizens living today. He was born in 1830 and died in 1892. James Major is to be remembered especially as a fine shoemaker, whose patrons included most of the prominent people of the town. It is said that his skill at shoemaking extended to the point where he could make a shoe to fit the special needs of a sore foot. A matter of interest for one today is the fact that during the Civil War this man made boots for $400 a pair in Confederate money. He maintained an illustrated "ad" in the city directory.

James Major Colson was married in 1852 to a free woman of color, Fannie Meade Bolling. His wife naturally was primarily a homemaker, but at the same time her literary attainments were manifested in her production of poetry throughout her long life. This lady came along during the period of the hostile legislation against the education of free Negroes. She learned to read and write at odd moments while in the employ of a white family that took great care that she should put her lessons aside in the event that company or strangers came into the home. Thus her very employers, regardless of the law, helped make it possible for her to acquire the rudiments of learning. Immediately after the war she put her knowledge to good use by taking the initiative in starting a private school on Oak Street in Petersburg.[158]

Among the numerous children of James Major Colson and Fannie Meade Colson, there were nine—three boys and six girls —who reached adult age. Six members of this family became teachers, while two of the boys entered skilled occupations, and one of the girls became a registered nurse. One of the boys, James Major III, who was born in 1855, completed Dartmouth College, where he received the Phi Beta Kappa key. He served as a school

[157]Ibid., pp. 372-73.
[158]Ibid., p. 377.

principal and for awhile as president of the Negro college in Petersburg. When he died in 1909 he left his family a fairly considerable amount of real estate. The five children of James Major III have carried on the traditions of the family. Among them we find one, who after serving as an officer in the World War helped to establish the chief radical Negro magazine and graduated from the Columbia University Law School just before his untimely death. One daughter, who received her master's degree at the University of Chicago, has given promise of a distinguished career in social work, while another, who is working on her doctorate at Columbia University, is teaching in the school where her father was president.

In another place the writer has described the career of one of the free families that migrated from Fredericksburg, Virginia, in order to escape the restrictions placed upon this class.[159] Later he will show how these families which migrated to the North formed a part of the nucleus of free families that have conserved and passed on the highest ideals of family life.

As we go northward we find in Baltimore a large group of free Negro families. In 1860 there were among them 348 property holders, ten of whom were assessed at $5,000 or more.[160] In one of the leading savings banks where there were 206 Negro depositors in 1860, the average savings amounted to $126.97.[161] Although the amount of property per capita for the entire population was small, it was considerable in the case of thrifty individuals who laid the foundation for further development. It was in this group that Frederick Douglass was welcomed when he escaped from slavery. His daughter writes:

> The free people of Baltimore had their own circles from which the slaves were excluded. The ruling of them out of their society resulted more from the desire of the slaveholder than from any great wish of the free people themselves. If a slave would dare to hazard all danger and enter among the free people he would be received. To such a little circle of free people—a circle a little more exclusive than others, Frederick Baily was welcomed. Anna Murray, to whom he had given his

[159]E. Franklin Frazier, *The Negro Family in Chicago* (Chicago, 1932), pp. 235-37.
[160]James M. Wright, *The Free Negro in Maryland* (New York and London, 1921), p. 186.
[161]Ibid., p. 193.

heart, sympathized with him, and she devoted all her energies to assist him. The three weeks prior to the escape were busy and anxious weeks for Anna Murray. She had lived with the Wells family so long and, having been able to save the greater part of her earnings, was willing to share with the man she loved that he might gain the freedom he yearned to possess. Her courage, her sympathy at the start was the mainspring that supported the career of Frederick Douglass. As is the condition of most wives, her identity became so merged with that of her husband, that few of their earlier friends in the North really knew and appreciated the full value of the woman who presided over the Douglass home for forty-four years. When the escaped slave and future husband of Anna Murray had reached New York in safety, his first act was to write her of his arrival, and as they had previously arranged, she was to come on immediately. Reaching New York a week later, they were married and immediately took their wedding trip to New Bedford.[162]

The story of the origin and later history of one of the free families was given by one of the descendants who has taught in the public schools of Chicago long enough to receive a pension.

During the Revolution in San Domingo, my great-grandfather, on my father's side, a Scotchman, and his wife, a French woman, were forced to flee from the island because of the revolt of the Negroes against the whites and mulattoes. They had got down to the boat when the wife, leaving the two girls with their father, returned to the house to get something she had left. She was overtaken by the black soldiers at the top of the hill. They captured her and decapitated her. During the excitement caused by the appearance of the soldiers one of the children disappeared. When the boat reached Baltimore my great-grandfather decided that he would go back to Scotland and find his people. So he left his little girl with the nurse they had brought with them from Haiti. When he got to Scotland he died. This child was therefore left in Baltimore with the colored mammy and reared as a colored child. I have now in my possession a daguerreotype taken of her when she was between sixty and seventy.

When she grew to be a woman she married a man named Jones, whose mother came from Guinea. They had fifteen children. Everyone was given a trade. They were apprenticed to someone. They were members of the Methodist church and owned their home on Mott Street in Baltimore. Uncle D— was a painter; Uncle W— was a harness maker; Uncle L— was a blacksmith; and several of them were coopers. Aunt L— married a man named G— G—, and had a large farm. He specialized in raising celery and sold it in the markets of Baltimore. Aunt J— was a mattress maker. She showed considerable skill in this art. She collected all the family heirlooms and kept them. When she was old and realized she was going to die, she distributed

them among the family. I received a medal, which had been awarded
to her by Rev. D. A. Payne, who later became bishop in the A. M. E.,
for the "2nd best piece of Embroidery at the 1st. Lit. and Artistic
Demonstration among People of Color in U. W. A. February 25th,
1850." Uncle D— was sworn over to keep the peace and never strike
a man with his fist because he was so large. All my aunts and uncles
were tall, showing their Scottish descent. They were all very self-
willed. One uncle went to San Francisco and married there and had
three girls.[163]

After the failure of John Brown's raid this woman's father
joined a group of free Negroes who went to Haiti. When he
returned he went to Chatham, Canada, where many free Negroes
had sought a refuge after the passage of the Fugitive Slave Law.
There he met and married the mother of our informant, who was
of Pennsylvania German and Indian mixture. As the remainder
of the history of this family would take us into the North, we
shall end it at this point and turn to the free Negro families in
Philadelphia.

In 1841 a southern observer of the free colored people of
Philadelphia wrote as follows:

> Taking the whole body of the colored population in the city of
> Philadelphia, they present in a gradual, moderate, and limited ratio,
> almost every grade of character, wealth, and—I think it not too much
> to add—of education. They are to be seen in ease, comfort and the en-
> joyment of all the social blessings of this life; and, in contrast with this,
> they are to be found in the lowest depths of human degradation, mis-
> ery, and want. They are also presented in the intermediate stages—
> sober, honest, industrious and respectable—claiming neither "poverty
> nor riches," yet maintaining, by their pursuits, their families in com-
> parative ease and comfort, oppressed neither with the cares of the rich,
> nor assailed by the deprivation and suffering of the indigent. The same
> in these respects that may be said of any other class of people, may,
> with the utmost regard to truth, be said of them.[164]

[163]*Manuscript document.* See also Wright, op. cit., Chap. IV, concerning the apprenticeship
of Negro children.
[164]*Sketches of the Higher Classes of Colored Society in Philadelphia*, by a Southerner (Philadelphia,
1841), pp. 14-15. The author says in regard to the title: "The prejudiced reader, I feel well assured,
will smile at the designation 'higher classes of colored society.' The public—or at least the great
body, who have not been at the pains to make an examination—have long been accustomed to
regard the people of color as one consolidated mass, all huddled together, without any particular
or general distinctions, social or otherwise. The sight of one colored man with them, whatever may
be his apparent condition (provided it is anything but genteel!), is the sight of a community; and
the errors and crimes of one is adjudged as the criterion of character of the whole body." p. 13.

The community of free Negroes in Philadelphia had for some time carried on efforts for the improvement of the moral and social status of the Negro. These efforts found expression in the Free African Society, organized in 1787, out of which the African Protestant Episcopal Church and the African Methodist Episcopal Church developed.[165]

Many of the families in Philadelphia had migrated from the South because of the persecution of the free Negro after 1830.[166] This was the case with a family that originated in Charleston, S. C. The history of this family begins with a full-blooded Indian woman who bought a fine-looking Negro as soon as he was landed with a slave cargo and emancipated him in order that he might marry her daughter.[167] From this union there was a daughter who became the mother of six children, the father of whom was a Scotchman. The story of this family continues:

> When the mother of these six children died, the Scotchman, before marrying an old maid who was white, took his children before the altar of his church and acknowledged his paternity. My grandmother, S—, used to tell us that she remembered standing at the altar with her brothers and sisters. This Scotch old maid sewed and took care of the colored children as long as she lived, although they did not live at the same house with her. S—'s brother kept up his friendship with his father's relatives in Scotland, and it was while on a visit there that he died. He is buried in a Scottish graveyard. One of these six children was my grandmother, S—. S— fell in love with a slave by the name of C—. The old Indian great-grandmother who ruled the whole family, including several generations, made C—, who married my grandmother, buy his freedom before she would permit him to marry her great-granddaughter. I have still, in my family, the document stating that my grandmother had always been free.[168]

Free ancestry and devotion to freedom have formed an im-

[165]We have an example of the efforts of this organization to control the conduct of its members and maintain standards in the following action of the Society. "Whereas, Samuel S., one of the members of the Free African Society, held in Philadelphia, for the benefit of the sick, has so shamefully deviated from our known rules, hath often, unnecessarily, left his tender wife and child, and kept company with a common woman, sometimes quarreling, fighting and swearing, for which he hath been long and tenderly treated with, but he has not forsaken his shameful practices, we therefore disown the said Samuel S. from being a member of our society till he condemns the same in life and conversation, which is our desire for him." George F. Bragg, *History of the Afro-American Group of the Episcopal Church*, pp. 55-56.

[166]See Carter G. Woodson, *A Century of Negro Migration* (Washington, 1918), passim.

[167]See Frazier, op. cit., pp. 232-34.

[168]*Manuscript document*, quoted in Frazier, op. cit., p. 232.

portant part in the memories and traditions which have been passed down in this family. Her story continued:

> When grandmother S— married C— they went to live on a little farm outside of Charleston. They must have prospered, for they seemingly had a good competence. A story has come down in our family exemplifying their devotion to the principles of human freedom. When grandmother S— sold her first calf and was asked what she was going to do with the money, she said she was going to buy a female slave. Her husband, C—, was so set against slavery that he almost struck her. The family moved into the city of Charleston and conducted the largest tailoring establishment in the city. During the slavery agitation my grandfather was walking with his son one day down the street, and a white man struck him with a cane. He had been insulted on several occasions, but this was the last straw. They sold out everything and went to X (a northern city). Men, coming out of the South, came to the home of my widowed grandmother to pay their respects because they had learned their trade in the shop of my grandfather.[169]

In Philadelphia the family continued in the words of our informant "to uphold our traditions." This following significant statement which is included gives an insight into the distinctions which were recognized by these free families.

> The people there regarded all mulatto women from the South as the illegitimate children of white men, but in the case of our family we could boast of being legitimate.[170]

The children in this family were educated at the Institute for Colored Youth, which was presided over by the first colored graduate of Oberlin College.

It was to Philadelphia that another Negro family of prominence made its way before the Civil War. The origin of this family is given as follows:

> James Yates, a Scotchman, died in the early part of the eighteenth century. He had no children. To a slave, Julia Cromwell, and her two daughters he left, by his will, their freedom and two of his seven plantations. They were cheated of their freedom, and the entire estate was devoted to the use of free schools for poor whites. The posterity of the three were known as the "Free School Negroes." My father, Willis H. Cromwell, was the great-grandson of July or Judy Cromwell, being born in 1792 the son of Hodges and Esther Cromwell.[171]

[169]*Manuscript document*, quoted in Frazier, op. cit., p. 233.
[170]*Manuscript document*, quoted in Frazier, op. cit., p. 234.
[171]Quoted in Notes, *The Journal of Negro History*, Vol. XII, p. 563.

Other facts concerning the history of the family are told by Woodson.

> Deprived of his lawful heritage of freedom, Willis Cromwell, with the assistance of his wife, ran a freight ferry boat after hours between Norfolk and Portsmouth, and by this means accumulated enough money to purchase from the "Free School Estate" himself, his wife, his six children, and his son-in-law. Thus freed, the entire family moved to Philadelphia in 1851. The papers of purchase pertaining to the sales are in the possession of the Cromwell family, who cherish these documents with the same pride they take in the spirit of independence, the vision, and industry that made their grandfather, his wife and children free men before the Emancipation Proclamation was signed. To this concrete and effective protest against human bondage may be directly traced Mr. Cromwell's own love of liberty, expressing itself in his uncompromising advocacy of the rights of Negroes.
>
> The main facts of Mr. Cromwell's own life may be simply told. In Philadelphia he attended a private elementary school for Negroes and later the Institute for Colored Youth, being graduated in 1864. The Institute for Colored Youth was founded and maintained by the Quakers, and under the principalship of Professor Ebenezer Bassett was a type of the best American academies of its day. It offered to its students a broad and intensive training in the classics, mathematics, and history. Under the inspiration of the ideals of the institution, Mr. Cromwell became a close student of Greek, Latin, mathematics, history, and English, developing thereby a love of books that was to remain his predominant characteristic throughout life.
>
> After graduation he taught school in Columbia, Pennsylvania, Wytheville and Richmond, Virginia, becoming at the same time a potent force in the stirring political affairs of Reconstruction. On account of his outspoken activity in defending Negro rights, he was twice shot at in Columbia. At Richmond he was a member of the jury empaneled to try Jefferson Davis.
>
> In 1871 he came to Washington to accept a clerkship in the departmental service of the Federal Government. While in this service, Mr. Cromwell began the study of law at Howard University and completed the course in 1874. He practiced law and subsequently edited and published a weekly newspaper, *The People's Advocate.* In 1889 he returned to the schoolroom and for thirty years was a teacher in the Public Schools of the District of Columbia. After his retirement from teaching, he spent his time chiefly in writing. He died on April 14, 1927.[172]

Probably it is not due to an accident that a talented Negro actor and singer, who has shown himself equally capable in scholarship and athletics, is a descendant of one of these free

[172]Ibid., Vol. XII, pp. 563-64.

families in Philadelphia.[173]   The history of the family as told by one of the descendants living in Chicago runs as follows:

> Cyrus Bustill, the most prominent of this family, was born in Burlington, New Jersey, February 2, 1732. He learned the art of bread-making from a well-known Quaker named Thomas Prior. One of the streets running to the fast flowing Delaware was named for him. Probably his bake-shop was located upon it. He went into business for himself and established quite a profitable trade.
>
> He always championed the cause of freedom and gave of his means to promote it. He "would not perpetuate a race of slaves;" so he did not marry early in life. Finally he married Elizabeth Morey, daughter of Satterthwait, an Indian maiden of the Delaware tribe, who lived on the banks of the nigh river bearing their name, and with whom William Penn made his famous treaty for "Penn's Woods." She was as free as himself, and both were familiar with the manners and customs of the Friends. They reared a family of eight children, Rachel, Mary, Ruth, Leah, Grace, Charles, Cyrus, and David.
>
> Cyrus Bustill, as the records will show, conducted his bread, cake, and biscuit business many years with credit and profit. (He was employed in supplying bread to the Revolutionary soldiers.) This was a patriotic contribution to the struggle of the Continental Forces. It is said he received a silver piece as a souvenir, from General George Washington. A member of the family still preserves it.
>
> Cyrus moved to Philadelphia, and still conducted his baking business at 56 Arch Street. His daughter, Grace, who lived next door and conducted a Quaker millinery store, had for customers some of the best families.
>
> Cyrus early became convinced of the rectitude of Friends' principles, and conformed to their mode of garb and speech. Not only did he conform outwardly, but Richard Prior, son of Thomas Prior, informed his granddaughter, Sarah M. Douglass, that "his deportment was solid and edifying, and that the inner man was transformed by renewing of the Holy Ghost." Cyrus and his family attended the Fourth and Arch meeting.
>
> He was sought for advice and aid in matters pertaining to the betterment of his race. He belonged to several benevolent societies of Philadelphia, especially the Free African Society founded April 12, 1787, which was a potent factor in the affairs of people of color of that day. In the annals of the first African Church in United States, the Protestant Episcopal Church of St. Thomas, 1862, it is said: "Cyrus Bustill was generally respected for his uprightness, and much relied upon by his brethren for his sound judgment. He was the first to relinquish his claim in the old Society in behalf of the church. This noble act appears to good advantage in view of his religious sentiments, which accorded with those of the Friends."
>
> He finally retired from business and built a house on Third and

[173]Eslanda Goode Robeson, *Paul Robeson, Negro* (New York, 1930), pp. 10-13.

Green Streets, where he opened a school and taught. The writer has a letter addressed to him as "school master" near Green Street, June 9, 1797. There were but poor chances for the education of the youth of his day, but despite all impediments, he was noted as a clear thinker and excellent writer, as sketches, a diary, and accounts still attest. He was an admirable speaker and a business man of considerable intelligence and experience.[174]

The great-grandchildren of Cyrus Bustill were typical of those Negroes who assimilated Quaker traditions. One of them, Sarah Mapps Douglass, who taught in the Philadelphia schools for sixty years, was connected with the Institute for Colored Youth. One of the cousins of Sarah Douglass married Reverend William D. Robeson, who in 1860, when he was fifteen years of age, escaped from slavery in North Carolina and worked his way through Lincoln University in Pennsylvania.[175]

In New York and the New England states many of the free families traced their origin back to soldiers who had fought in the Revolution. Concerning the free Negroes who participated in the Revolution, Hartgrove writes:

> A Hessian officer observed in 1777 that "the Negro can take the field instead of his master; and, therefore, no regiment is to be seen in which there are not negroes in abundance, and among them there are ablebodied, strong and brave fellows. "Here too," said he, "there are many families of free negroes who live in good homes, have property and live just like the rest of the inhabitants.[176]

The grandfather of a free Negro, who became the pastor of a church in Philadelphia, took the place of his master with the promise that when he returned he should receive his freedom. However, the promise was broken when the war was over. The grandson wrote as follows concerning the traditions of these soldiers which became part of his own heritage.

> There were in the town where Gad Asher resided two other colored soldiers of the Revolution, who were frequently accustomed to talk over the motives which prompted them to "endure hardness." They were the only men that I knew (and I was acquainted with nearly every man in the town) that fought in the terrible and never-to-be-forgotten battle for American Liberty. I was so accustomed to hear these men

[174]The Bustill Family, *The Journal of Negro History*, Vol. X, pp. 638-39.
[175]Robeson, op. cit., p. 10.
[176]W. B. Hartgrove, Negro Soldier in American Revolution, *Journal of Negro History*, Vol. I, p. 126.

talk, until I almost fancied to myself that I had more rights than any white man in the town. Such were the lessons taught me by the old black soldiers of the American Revolution. Thus, my first ideas of the right of the colored man to life, liberty and the pursuit of happiness were received from those old veterans and champions for liberty.[177]

In some cases these families have nothing in their background in common with the masses of Negroes. The traditions of these families are those of white and sometimes Indian ancestors, while their blood relationship with Negroes has been established through intermarriage with mulattoes. One of these families traces its origin back to a soldier who served in the Revolution and was present at Valley Forge with Washington. He was married to Charity Wainwright, the sister of Bishop Wainwright of England. Their grandson married a woman of English, Spanish, and Indian mixture and settled on Long Island. A son by this union married the daughter of a mulatto slave, celebrated in a poem by an American poet, and thus introduced Negro blood into the family. A daughter, one of the six children by this marriage, said:

> I have the sewing bird that Charity Wainwright, who was the only weaver in Connecticut during her day, used. We also have the candlesticks and snuffers that they made candles in, as well as the table that grandmother had during the Revolutionary War, and hid money in from the British soldiers. In my living room we have the furniture that has been in the family five generations. It is solid bronze.[178]

Charles Dickens in his *American Notes*[179] has given the world a picture of the degradation of the Negro in New York City. Probably a black Negro woman weighing 350 pounds and "known variously as Big Sue and the Turtle," who kept a dive in the Arch Block, is better known to history[180] than Thomas Downing, the proprietor of a restaurant on Broad Street, or the owner of Fraunces' Tavern, where George Washington gave his farewell dinner to his officers in 1783.[181] But the latter two are typical of

---

[177]Jeremiah Asher, *An Autobiography with details of a visit to England* (Philadelphia, 1862), p. 5.
[178]*Manuscript document.*
[179]See Herbert Asbury, *The Gangs of New York* (New York, 1927), pp. 10-12.
[180]Ibid., p. 47.
[181]James Weldon Johnson, *Black Manhattan* (New York, 1930), pp. 44-45. Woodson, *The Negro in Our History*, 5th edition (Washington, 1928), p. 255. Woodson, *A Century of Negro Migration*, p. 87.

the Negroes of New York who secured some economic competency and became a part of the vanguard of the race in its cultural development. The descendants of Downing have built upon the beginnings of their ancestor and their status in the Negro world today reflects these advantages.

Among the Negroes in New York City who became the sources of family lines which we can trace to the present day was James Varick, one of the founders and later the first bishop of the African Methodist Episcopal Zion Church.[182] His biographer gives his history as follows:

> Richard Varick, who was of Dutch descent, the father of James Varick, was born in Hackensack, New Jersey, but when a child moved with his parents to New York City. It is difficult to tell to what nationality James Varick belongs. At least three different nationalities enter into his composition. Through his veins flowed the blood of the Negro, the American Indian, and the Dutchman. According to the American way of settling race identity, I suppose he would be called a Negro, for he had Negro blood flowing through his veins. . . . . The exact date of Varick's birth is not clearly known, but, putting all the facts in his eventful life together, it appears that 1750 is as near a date as can be given as the year of his birth. . . . . He was born in stirring times when the best brains and the best blood were all aflame with a desire for liberty, which was expressed twenty-six years after his birth in the Declaration of Independence of English rule. Varick caught the spirit of his age and in due time was ready to lead his little band of followers to religious liberty. Just *where* Varick was born is not clearly known. It is stated by the early fathers of the church that he was born in Newburg, N. Y., up the Hudson river from New York City. While Varick was born in Newburg, it appears that his mother was a resident of New York and was in Newburg on a visit when Varick was born. At any rate, James Varick was reared in New York City. His mother was a colored woman of very bright complexion. Whether she had been a slave or was a free woman is not known. In the history of New York city the rich and distinguished Varick family has figured most conspicuously in its social, political and commercial life for the last two centuries. One of the members of this cultured Varick family was mayor of New York city. The Varick Bank of New York city is named in honor of, and controlled by this same strong and influential family. Varick street on which I have walked many times, which runs from Clarkson street to Canal, is also named after this distinguished family. It is possible that Varick's mother at one time was a slave in the family.[183]

[182]Woodson, *The Negro in Our History*, p. 152.
[183]B. F. Wheeler, *The Varick Family* ([Mobile, 1906]), pp. 8-9.

As a child James Varick took advantage of the educational
opportunities offered Negroes and became a shoemaker.   He
was influenced by the preaching of Phillip Embury and Captain
Thomas Webb and joined the John Street Methodist Church.[184]
It appears that Varick married around 1798 when he was forty-
eight years old.   There were four children, two boys and two
girls. Of the youngest child we have the following account:

> Mary Varick was the youngest child of James Varick and Aurelia
> Jones. She, like her aunt, Emeline, was highly cultured, being one of the
> intellectual women of New York City in her day. She was secretary of
> most of the organizations among Negroes in the city of New York in
> her day. At the time of her death she was secretary of the North Star
> Association, an organization which had for its purpose the booming of
> Frederick Douglass, the rising young orator of the Negro race at that
> time. She married Robert Cromwell. Robert Cromwell was a distin-
> guished colored man, and well deserved to become the husband of one
> of the daughters of Bishop Varick. First of all, he was well educated.
> In the second place, he owned considerable property. His property
> holdings for the most part were in New Haven, Conn. He was a most
> exemplary man in many other respects. He never tasted a drop of
> liquor, nor used tobacco in any form. He was upright in all of his bus-
> iness dealings with his fellowmen. His word was his bond. He was
> authority on Masonic matters. And in the lodge he is said to have been
> a strict disciplinarian. He was devoted to his wife, and their married
> life was congenial and happy. Seven children were born to them.[185]

By 1906 the five generations of descendants of James Varick
had numbered forty: four children; sixteen grandchildren; thirteen great-grandchildren; five great-great-grandchildren; and one
great-great-great-grandchild.[186]

Another Negro bishop who was born in slavery and after
escaping made his way to Syracuse, New York, also became the
head of a family line extending down to the present day. Bishop
Loguen was born in Tennessee of a Negro mother and white
father.[187]   His mother when seven years of age had been kid-
napped in Ohio and carried into Kentucky, and later sold to
three brothers near Nashville, Tennessee. The youngest of these
brothers later took her as his mistress. Although his father had

[184]Ibid., p. 11.
[185]Ibid., pp. 29-30.
[186]Ibid., p. 34.
[187]*The Rev. J. W. Loguen as a Slave and as a Freeman* (Syracuse, N. Y., 1859), pp. 12-25.

promised his mother that their three children should be emancipated, they were sold into slavery to satisfy a debt. He succeeded in escaping from slavery and made his way to Canada. Later he settled in Syracuse, where he had charge of the Underground Railroad. He was married in 1840. There were three children, one of whom became a physician and another a portrait artist. The son of the latter followed the career of his father, while the great-grandson of the bishop is at present a senior in college.

We have already referred to the settlements of free Negroes in the Northwest Territory and other rural communities of the North. In the remainder of this essay we shall trace the origin and career of several of the free families which issued from these communities. Perhaps the most celebrated of these communities was the Gouldtown Settlement in New Jersey. As the writer has given in another place a full account of this family, he will only give some of the outstanding facts here.[188] The traditions of this mulatto community extend back to the seventeenth century. According to the tradition this community originated with the marriage of a Negro to the granddaughter of John Fenwick who, having acquired from Lord Berkley a tract of land in New Jersey, came to America in 1775.[189] This settlement was comprised of three other families of mulatto and Indian extraction. One of them originated with two mulatto brothers from the West Indies who married Dutch women, whose passages they had paid from Holland. The second family sprang from a man of Indian descent who married a Swedish woman; while the third family, which intermarried with the three original families, was the descendants of a slave who later married the widow of his master.

---

[188]Cf. Frazier, *The Negro Family in Chicago,* pp. 41-45.

[189]William Steward and Theophilus G. Steward, *Gouldtown, a Very Remarkable Settlement of Ancient Date* (Philadelphia, 1913), pp. 50-51. "Among the numerous troubles and vexations which assailed Fenwick, none appear to have distressed him more than the base and abandoned conduct of his granddaughter, Elizabeth Adams, who had attached herself to a citizen of color. By his will he deprives her of any share in his estate, 'unless the Lord open her eyes to see her abominable transgression against him, me and her good father, by giving her true repentance and forsaking that Black, which hath been the ruin of her and becoming penitent for her sins.' From this illicit connection have sprung the families of the Goulds at a settlement called Gouldtown, in Cumberland County. Later, this same historian in a memoir of John Fenwick wrote: "Elizabeth Adams had formed a connection with a negro man whose name was Gould'." (R. G. Johnson, *Memoir of John Fenwick,* in New Jersey Historical Society [published 1849].)

Descendants of the families who made up this settlement have played conspicuous roles in Negro life. One helped to organize the African Methodist Church in Philadelphia. Although it is impossible to catalogue the attainments of all the descendants of these free families, we can indicate in a way the extent of their influence by recording the fact that when the annual reunion was celebrated in 1910 there were two hundred and twenty-three living descendants of one grandson of Benjamin Gould I, whose mother was the granddaughter of John Fenwick.[190] Several members of these families intermarried with whites and their descendants passed over into the white race. Among the members of these families who remained in the Negro race we find a bishop, an army chaplain, a physician, a lawyer, teachers, writers, journalists, machinists, engineers, electricians, and ministers of the gospel.[191]

From another mulatto settlement, in Indiana, have come families that have attained similar distinction in the Negro group. According to the story told by a descendant of two of these families, his paternal grandfather, who was of Indian and Negro extraction, was born free in North Carolina in 1795. Together with his four brothers he came with other families to Indiana between 1823 and 1825 because they were forced by the whites to leave North Carolina. Before leaving North Carolina he had purchased and married in 1816 a mulatto slave who was the daughter of an American general. There were twelve children— seven boys and five girls. The children were reared on the eighty acre farm which their father had bought upon coming to Indiana. All of the children became farmers or farmers' wives, except one who went into the army. One of these children, the father of our informant, married a woman who was a descendant of a chief of an Indian tribe in Massachusetts. The son of this chief married an Irish woman, and their son, who was a sort of a wanderer, went to North Carolina. There he married a mulatto woman, who gave birth in 1823 to the maternal grandfather of our in-

---

[190]Steward and Steward, op. cit., pp. 109-12.
[191]Ibid., p. 12.

formant. This family was also forced to leave the state of North Carolina. When this maternal grandfather reached manhood he married and became the father of nine children, whom he reared on his farm. One daughter was married to the father of our informant.

As in the case of the families in the New Jersey settlement, some members of the two families whose histories we have just given have gone into the white race. Likewise, others have achieved distinction in the Negro group. Among these we can enumerate physicians, school teachers, a legislator, and one member who received a federal appointment. We shall close the story of these families with the words of our informant, a distinguished physician on the staff of a white hospital.

> Our settlement was first established around 1823. The earliest tombstone bears the date 1827. My grandfather was buried in that cemetery in 1848. The settlement included about four or five square miles. There was a school and church. One of the stations on the Underground Railway was located there. Soil was very fertile. Racial relations were very good. They have had family reunions there for about thirty-seven years. At the present time only three or four of the original families are there. At one time we had as many as eight or nine hundred people gathered there at family reunions.[192]

A family whose history has been published recently begins thus:

> In the year 1754 a ship with a cargo of African slaves landed at Jamestown, Virginia; among them was a boy 10 years of age, a son of an African prince. This boy became the father of the family of whom we write, a family now scattered throughout many states of the Union. . . . .
> This boy grew to manhood without having to submit to the yoke of bondage. The only reason that can be assigned is that they had respect for the royal blood that was known to course through his veins. This may or may not be true, but this we know, that he nor none of his posterity were ever held as slaves.[193]

When this reputed son of an African prince grew to manhood he apparently married a free woman, since his children were also free. The historian of the family continues:

[192]*Manuscript document.*
[193]John L. Jones, *History of the Jones Family* (Greenfield, Ohio, [1930?]), pp. 9-10.

I do not know the number of children born to this first family. My father told us the story more than once, but I cannot say with certainty as to his uncles; he spoke more often of his father, who was a son of this pair, and whose name was Ruben Jones. Ruben Jones was born in Henrico County, Virginia, in 1795.[194]

Reuben Jones married a free woman. The story goes:

There was in this neighborhood a family by the name of All-stock; the father was an Englishman—the mother was an Indian squaw. Besides father and mother there were three girls, two of whom were white, taking their complexion from their father; the other girl was of a little darker hue. The two white ones married white men and were lost in the white race. The girl of darker hue married Ruben Jones. These sisters went in opposite directions and never met each other again.[195]

The life of the family that issued from this marriage is described as follows:

Reuben Jones and wife were Christians; the wife was loved and respected for her devoted life and Christian integrity. They had four children, John, Joseph, Mary and Martha. They must have had some knowledge of the Bible, else whence these names? The colored people of this community had a church of some description of which Reuben and wife were members. I have often heard my father tell of the time that he, when a small boy, was refused membership in the church because when giving in his experience he did not see the devil nor hear any chains rattle, neither did he go to the graveyard to pray at midnight. That was enough. He was sent back and told that he did not have the genuine religion.

These boys were put to work at an early age. At 10, Joseph was given a team; he made a round trip to Richmond every day with a load of cord-wood—a distance of 10 miles. Wood was in great demand and the only fuel available for domestic purposes. This wood was sold for cash and the proceeds turned over to the father every night less three cents, the liberal allowance given the boy for lunch. The lunch consisted of bread 1c, molasses 2c. After finishing this splendid repast he would start on his return trip for home.[196]

Because of the hardships of these trips, Joseph, with the approval of his mother, left home.

Joseph had many advantages over his brother. In his daily trips to Richmond he had contact with people, and in that way learned among other things the way to complete freedom; through this contact

---

[194]Ibid., p. 10.   In Woodson's *Free Negro Heads of Families in the United States in 1830*, p. 176 there is listed for Henrico County a Reuben Jones.   This is apparently the same person.
[195]Ibid., p. 11.
[196]Ibid., pp. 12-13.

he figured out his way to Ohio. With the approval of his mother and the kindly advice of friends he gathered together his belongings, wrapped them up in a red bandana handkerchief, and in the quiet of the night he silently stole away.

This journey for a boy just 13 was not without hazard. The distance to Ohio was about 400 miles through an unbroken country, and at that time the mountains were said to have wild beasts in plenty. Again he was traveling without free papers; he either forgot them or did not know that they were necessary. All free Negroes could get free papers from the county court house with the county seal affixed, so in case of question they could show their papers and pass on, otherwise they could be arrested by any white man and sold into slavery. He made his escape and finally landed on the bank of the Kanawha River near Point Pleasant in sight of the state of Ohio, his objective. While standing there a steamboat came down the river; he waved at the boat. The captain took it for a signal to land; bringing his boat to land he asked the boy what he wanted. To which he replied, "Do you need any men on this boat?" The captain ordered the stage plank lowered, and the boy went aboard. This boat was bound for Cincinnati, Ohio, with this new boy, working at a new job in a new world.[197]

For awhile Joseph continued to work on the boat. When the boat was laid up during the winter months he remained aboard with the captain, who for three years gave him instruction. At the end of this time he took up his residence in Cincinnati, where he found a place in the Negro community through membership in the largest Negro Baptist church in the city. He worked as a cooper and whitewasher, and returned to the boat at times. He married into one of the families settled in southern Ohio and located in Gallipolis, where he organized a singing school as well as carried on his business as a cooper. His was one of the colored families that employed a teacher to teach their children in the first school for colored children in Gallipolis. One of Joseph's children was the historian of the family, who was born in 1857. The members of the family who had been left in Virginia joined Joseph's family in Ohio as soon as communication could be established.

Brother John sold the farm and came to Ohio, bringing his parents and sisters with him. They landed at Gallipolis and were directed to the home of their son and brother. They were received midst tears and

[197]Ibid., pp. 14-15.

laughter, Grandmother Jones resting on the breast of her favorite son, wept copiously. Many a hallelujah and praise God went up from the lips of all. This is the answer to twenty years of prayer; this is the faith that believes in waiting on the Lord.

Father and Mother Jones were old and broken in health; they had never known anything but hard work, for years they had been incapacitated, and all fell on Brother John. So Joseph was glad to be in a position to take his father and mother and keep them for the remainder of their days. So far as the money from the sale of the home is concerned, take it and use it to give yourself and the girls a start in life. I will look after mother and father to the end. After visiting with his brother for several weeks, John went to Ross county and bought a farm. Land was cheap at that time, not over 15c or 20c per acre. He raised two sets of children and became well-to-do. His farm, consisting of 240 acres, is still in the hands of his children.[198]

The home of this family served, like those of other free Negro families, as a station of the Underground Railroad. As space will not permit us to follow further the career of this family, we shall give a brief story of a Negro family that formed a part of the Negro community in Cass County, Michigan.

The story of this family was furnished by one of the descendants who has distinguished himself as an artist. The oldest known ancestor, a very light mulatto, was born in Richmond, Virginia about the year 1779. He migrated to Ohio, and in 1812 married a mulatto woman who had also come from Virginia, where she was born in 1794 or thereabout. The husband with his brothers carried on a prosperous tannery business in Chillicothe for a number of years. The couple had a large number of children, eleven of whom reached manhood and womanhood. In 1844 the family moved to Michigan and became a part of the community referred to at the beginning of this study.

We can not conclude our account of the families in the Northwest Territory without mentioning at least the small group of families which settled in Chicago and Detroit. In the former city Negroes have appeared in its chronicles from the time of the first settlers.[199] Some of these families prospered and formed an element in the Negro population that represented the advancement

---

[198]Ibid., p. 30.
[199]See Frazier, op. cit., pp. 86-87.

of the Negro in the North for many decades. For example, one of these families originated from free mulattoes and whites from New York and Ohio. The father of one of the descendants, who was born in Chicago in 1845, conducted a successful express business and owned property in what is now the Loop.

The community of free Negro families in Detroit was made up largely of families that migrated from Virginia. We have already given the origin of the Richards family. A description of the other families in this community has been given as follows:

> In this favorable community the Richards family easily prospered. The Lees well established themselves in their northern homes and soon won the respect of the community. Most of the members of the Williams family confined themselves to their trade of bricklaying and amassed considerable wealth. One of Mr. Williams' daughters married a well-to-do Waring living then at Wauseon, Ohio; another became the wife of one Chappee, who is now a stenographer in Detroit, and the third united in matrimony with James H. Cole, who became the head of a well-to-do family of Detroit. Then there were the Cooks, descending from Lomax B. Cook, a broker of no little business ability. The DeBaptistes, too, were among the first to get a foothold in this new environment and prospered materially from their experience and knowledge acquired in Fredericksburg as contractors. From this group came Richard DeBaptiste, who in his day was the most noted colored Baptist preacher in the Northwest. The Pelhams were no less successful in establishing themselves in the economic world. They enjoyed a high reputation in the community and had the sympathy and cooperation of the influential white people in the city. Out of this family came Robert A. Pelham, for years editor of a weekly in Detroit, and from 1871 to the present time an employee of the Federal Government in Washington[200]

These families complete our account of the families that took root in the free colored communities. Although these records do not approach anything like a comprehensive description and history of these families, they are typical of the free colored families in the seven characteristic areas where the free Negro flourished before the Civil War.

---

[200]Hartgrove, The Story of Maria Louise Moore and Fannie M. Richards, *Journal of Negro History*, Vol. I, pp. 23-33, quoted in Frazier, op. cit., p. 237.

CONCLUSION

Our study of the origin, growth, and distribution of the free Negroes before the Civil War has revealed the close relationship between the ecological organization of slavery and the emergence of this class. The restrictions which were placed upon the growth and development of this class were nullified more or less by the underlying material conditions. Moreover, we have seen how the free class grew through the association of the races in spite of the legal restrictions upon such relations. In the communities of free Negroes, who became segregated in seven characteristic areas, families took on an institutional character. Economic competency, culture, and achievement gave these families a special status and became the source of a tradition which has been transmitted to succeeding generations. These families have been the chief bearers of the first economic and cultural gains of the race, and have constituted a leavening element in the Negro population wherever they have been found. We have noted how frequently the descendants of these families are still found today in conspicuous places in the Negro world. Their achievements and status reflect the cultural and economic advantages of the families whose careers we have traced. Therefore, in studying the different problems of the Negro one must take into account these various cultural strains which, often unperceived, thread Negro life.

SELECTED BIBLIOGRAPHY

The books, articles, and documents listed below include only those published works which have been consulted for this study. The author has also drawn on a large number of documents which he has collected during his researches concerning the Negro family.

ALLEN, RICHARD. *The Life, Experience and Gospel Labors of the Rt. Richard Allen* (Philadelphia, 1830).

ASBURY, HERBERT. *The Gangs of New York* (New York, 1927).

ASHER, JEREMIAH. *An Autobiography with Details of a Visit to England* (Philadelphia, 1862).

BASSETT, JOHN SPENCER. *Slavery in the State of North Carolina* (Baltimore, 1899).
——————. *Anti-Slavery Leaders of North Carolina* (Baltimore, 1898).

BIRNIE, C. W. The Education of the Negro in Charleston, S. C. before the Civil War, *Journal of Negro History*, Vol. XII.

BOND, HORACE MANN. Two Racial Islands in Alabama, *American Journal of Sociology*, Vol. XXXVI.

BRACKETT, JEFFREY R. *The Negro in Maryland* (Baltimore, 1889).

BRAGG, GEORGE F. *History of the Afro-American Group of the Episcopal Church* (Baltimore, 1922).
——————. *Men of Maryland* (Baltimore, 1925).

BRAWLEY, BENJAMIN. *A Social History of the American Negro* (New York, 1921)

BUREAU OF THE CENSUS, Washington, D. C.
The Seventh Census of the United States: 1850.
Population of the United States in 1860.
Negro Population in the United States, 1790-1915.

CALHOUN, ARTHUR W. *A Social History of the American Family* (Cleveland, 1917).

CATTERALL, HELEN T. (ed.). *Judicial Cases Concerning American Slavery and the Negro* (Washington, 1926).

CHARLESTON. *List of Tax Payers of the City of Charleston for 1860.*

CORRUTHERS, JAMES D. *In Spite of Handicap, An Autobiography* (New York, 1916).

CROMWELL, JOHN W. The First Negro Churches in Washington, *Journal of Negro History*, Vol. VII.

DANIELS, JOHN. *In Freedom's Birthplace* (Boston, 1914).

DAVIS, NOAH. *The Narrative of the Life of Noah Davis, A Colored Man, Written by Himself at the Age of Fifty-Four* (Baltimore, 1859).

DESDUNES, R. L. *Nos Hommes et Notre histoire* (Montreal, 1911).

DODGE, DAVIS. The Free Negroes of North Carolina, *Atlantic Monthly*, Vol. LVII.

DuBois, W. E. BURGHARDT. *The Philadelphia Negro* (Philadelphia, 1899).

DUNBAR-NELSON, ALICE. *People of Color in Louisiana*, Part I. *Journal of Negro History*, Vol. I, 361-76; Part II, Vol. II, 51-78.

ESTABROOK, ARTHUR H. AND McDOUGLE, IVAN H. *Mongrel Virginians, The Win Tribe* (Baltimore, 1926).

FRAZIER, E. FRANKLIN. *The Negro Family in Chicago* (Chicago, 1932).

GREEN, JOHN P. *Fact Stranger Than Fiction* (Cleveland, 1920).

HARTGROVE, W. B. Negro Soldiers in American Revolution, *Journal of Negro History*, Vol. I.

HERRICK, CHEESEMAN A. *White Servitude in Pennsylvania* (Philadelphia, 1926).

JACKSON, LUTHER P. Free Negroes of Petersburg, Virginia, *Journal of Negro History*, Vol. XII.

JERVEY, THEODORE D. *The Slave Trade, Slavery and Color* (Columbia, S. C., 1925).

JOHNSON, CHARLES S. *The Negro in American Civilization* (New York, 1930).

JOHNSON, JAMES WELDON. *Black Manhattan* (New York, 1930).

JOHNSTON, J. H. Documentary Evidence of the Relations of Negroes and Indians, *Journal of Negro History*, Vol. XIV.

JONES, JOHN L. *History of the Jones Family* (Greenfield, Ohio, [1930?]).

Journal of Negro History, The
Anna Murray Douglass, My Mother As I Recall Her, Vol. VIII, pp. 93-98.
Concerning the Origin of Wilberforce, Vol. VIII, pp. 335-337.
Letter to Dr. Robert E. Park from an investigator in Ohio seeking information concerning the Randolph slaves, Vol. VII, pp. 207-211.
Notes, Vol. VII, pp. 563-66.
The Bustill Family, Vol. X, pp. 638-44.

KING, GRACE. *New Orleans, The Place and the People* (New York, 1928).

LANE, LUNSFORD. *The Narrative of Lunsford Lane, Formerly of Raleigh, N. C.* (Boston, 1842).

LOGUEN, J. W. *The Rev. J. W. Loguen as a Slave and as a Freeman* (Syracuse, N. Y., 1859).

Louisiana Under the Rule of Spain, France, and the United States, 1785-1807 (Cleveland, 1911).

Negro Year Book, 1931-1932.

OLMSTED, FREDERICK LAW. *A Journey in the Seaboard States in the Year 1853-1854* (New York, 1904).

PHILLIPS, ULRICH B. *American Negro Slavery* (New York, 1927).

—————. *Documentary History of American Industrial Society*, "Plantation and Frontier" (Cleveland, 1910).

REUTER, EDWARD BYRON. *The Mulatto in the United States* (Boston, 1918).

ROBESON, ESLANDA GOODE. *Paul Robeson, Negro* (New York, 1930).

RUSSELL, JOHN H. *The Free Negro in Virginia* (Baltimore, 1913).

SCHOOLCRAFT, H. B. *By a Southern Lady, Letters on the Condition of the African Race in the United States* (Philadelphia, 1852).

Sketches of the Higher Classes of Colored Society in Philadelphia, By a Southerner (Philadelphia, 1841).

SNYDOR, CHARLES S. The Free Negro in Mississippi Before the Civil War, *American Historical Review*, XXXII (July, 1927).

Statistical Inquiry into the Condition of the People of Colour, of the City and District of Philadelphia (Philadelphia, 1849).

STEWARD, WILLIAM AND STEWARD, THEOPHILUS G. *Gouldtown, a Very Remarkable Settlement of Ancient Date* (Philadelphia, 1913).

THOMAS, DAVID Y. The Free Negro in Florida Before 1865, *The South Atlantic Quarterly*, Vol. X.

TURNER, EDWARD RAYMOND. *The Negro in Pennsylvania* (Washington, 1911).

TURNER, HENRY M. *Life and Times of Henry M. Turner* (Atlanta, 1917).

WASHINGTON, BOOKER T. *The Story of the Negro* (New York, 1909).

WESLEY, CHARLES H. *Negro Labor in the United States: 1850-1925, A Study in American Economic History* (New York, 1927).

WHEELER, B. F. *The Varick Family* ([Mobile, 1906]).

WILLIAMS, GEORGE W. *History of the Negro Race in America* (New York, 1882).

WOODSON, CARTER G. *A Century of Negro Migration* (Washington, 1918).

—————. The Negroes of Cincinnati Prior to the Civil War, *Journal of Negro History*, Vol. I.

—————. *The Education of the Negro Prior to 1861* (New York and London, 1915).

—————. The Beginnings of the Miscegenation of Whites and Blacks, *Journal of Negro History*, Vol. III.

—————. *Free Negro Heads of Families in the United States in 1830* (Washington, D. C., 1925).

—————. The Relations of Negroes and Indians in Massachusetts, *Journal of Negro History*, Vol. V.

—————. *The Negro in Our History*, 5th edition (Washington, 1928).

—————. *Free Negro Owners of Slaves in the United States in 1830* (Washington, 1924).

—————. *The History of the Negro Church*, 2nd edition (Washington, 1921).

WRIGHT, JAMES M. *The Free Negro in Maryland* (New York and London, 1921).

Date Due